C-1010 CAREER EXAMINATION SERIES

This is your
PASSBOOK for...

Senior Investigator

Test Preparation Study Guide
Questions & Answers

NLC®

NATIONAL LEARNING CORPORATION®

COPYRIGHT NOTICE

This book is SOLELY intended for, is sold ONLY to, and its use is RESTRICTED to individual, bona fide applicants or candidates who qualify by virtue of having seriously filed applications for appropriate license, certificate, professional and/or promotional advancement, higher school matriculation, scholarship, or other legitimate requirements of education and/or governmental authorities.

This book is NOT intended for use, class instruction, tutoring, training, duplication, copying, reprinting, excerption, or adaptation, etc., by:

1) Other publishers
2) Proprietors and/or Instructors of "Coaching" and/or Preparatory Courses
3) Personnel and/or Training Divisions of commercial, industrial, and governmental organizations
4) Schools, colleges, or universities and/or their departments and staffs, including teachers and other personnel
5) Testing Agencies or Bureaus
6) Study groups which seek by the purchase of a single volume to copy and/or duplicate and/or adapt this material for use by the group as a whole without having purchased individual volumes for each of the members of the group
7) Et al.

Such persons would be in violation of appropriate Federal and State statutes.

PROVISION OF LICENSING AGREEMENTS – Recognized educational, commercial, industrial, and governmental institutions and organizations, and others legitimately engaged in educational pursuits, including training, testing, and measurement activities, may address request for a licensing agreement to the copyright owners, who will determine whether, and under what conditions, including fees and charges, the materials in this book may be used them. In other words, a licensing facility exists for the legitimate use of the material in this book on other than an individual basis. However, it is asseverated and affirmed here that the material in this book CANNOT be used without the receipt of the express permission of such a licensing agreement from the Publishers. Inquiries re licensing should be addressed to the company, attention rights and permissions department.

All rights reserved, including the right of reproduction in whole or in part, in any form or by any means, electronic or mechanical, including photocopying, recording, or by any information storage and retrieval system, without permission in writing from the Publisher.

Copyright © 2025 by
National Learning Corporation

212 Michael Drive, Syosset, NY 11791
(516) 921-8888 • www.passbooks.com
E-mail: info@passbooks.com

PASSBOOK® SERIES

THE *PASSBOOK® SERIES* has been created to prepare applicants and candidates for the ultimate academic battlefield – the examination room.

At some time in our lives, each and every one of us may be required to take an examination – for validation, matriculation, admission, qualification, registration, certification, or licensure.

Based on the assumption that every applicant or candidate has met the basic formal educational standards, has taken the required number of courses, and read the necessary texts, the *PASSBOOK® SERIES* furnishes the one special preparation which may assure passing with confidence, instead of failing with insecurity. Examination questions – together with answers – are furnished as the basic vehicle for study so that the mysteries of the examination and its compounding difficulties may be eliminated or diminished by a sure method.

This book is meant to help you pass your examination provided that you qualify and are serious in your objective.

The entire field is reviewed through the huge store of content information which is succinctly presented through a provocative and challenging approach – the question-and-answer method.

A climate of success is established by furnishing the correct answers at the end of each test.

You soon learn to recognize types of questions, forms of questions, and patterns of questioning. You may even begin to anticipate expected outcomes.

You perceive that many questions are repeated or adapted so that you can gain acute insights, which may enable you to score many sure points.

You learn how to confront new questions, or types of questions, and to attack them confidently and work out the correct answers.

You note objectives and emphases, and recognize pitfalls and dangers, so that you may make positive educational adjustments.

Moreover, you are kept fully informed in relation to new concepts, methods, practices, and directions in the field.

You discover that you are actually taking the examination all the time: you are preparing for the examination by "taking" an examination, not by reading extraneous and/or supererogatory textbooks.

In short, this PASSBOOK®, used directedly, should be an important factor in helping you to pass your test.

SENIOR INVESTIGATOR

DUTIES

As a Senior Investigator, you would conduct complex and sensitive investigations. Duties include conducting interviews and obtaining sworn statements from investigative targets and other witnesses, collecting and processing evidence, documenting investigative findings by writing narrative reports, testifying at administrative and criminal proceedings, and possible supervising subordinate staff.

SCOPE OF THE EXAMINATION

The written test will cover knowledge, skills and/or abilities in such areas as:

1. Advanced investigative techniques;
2. Evaluating information and evidence;
3. Investigative techniques;
4. Preparing written material;
5. Supervision; and
6. Understanding and interpreting written material.

HOW TO TAKE A TEST

I. YOU MUST PASS AN EXAMINATION

A. *WHAT EVERY CANDIDATE SHOULD KNOW*

Examination applicants often ask us for help in preparing for the written test. What can I study in advance? What kinds of questions will be asked? How will the test be given? How will the papers be graded?

As an applicant for a civil service examination, you may be wondering about some of these things. Our purpose here is to suggest effective methods of advance study and to describe civil service examinations.

Your chances for success on this examination can be increased if you know how to prepare. Those "pre-examination jitters" can be reduced if you know what to expect. You can even experience an adventure in good citizenship if you know why civil service exams are given.

B. *WHY ARE CIVIL SERVICE EXAMINATIONS GIVEN?*

Civil service examinations are important to you in two ways. As a citizen, you want public jobs filled by employees who know how to do their work. As a job seeker, you want a fair chance to compete for that job on an equal footing with other candidates. The best-known means of accomplishing this two-fold goal is the competitive examination.

Exams are widely publicized throughout the nation. They may be administered for jobs in federal, state, city, municipal, town or village governments or agencies.

Any citizen may apply, with some limitations, such as the age or residence of applicants. Your experience and education may be reviewed to see whether you meet the requirements for the particular examination. When these requirements exist, they are reasonable and applied consistently to all applicants. Thus, a competitive examination may cause you some uneasiness now, but it is your privilege and safeguard.

C. *HOW ARE CIVIL SERVICE EXAMS DEVELOPED?*

Examinations are carefully written by trained technicians who are specialists in the field known as "psychological measurement," in consultation with recognized authorities in the field of work that the test will cover. These experts recommend the subject matter areas or skills to be tested; only those knowledges or skills important to your success on the job are included. The most reliable books and source materials available are used as references. Together, the experts and technicians judge the difficulty level of the questions.

Test technicians know how to phrase questions so that the problem is clearly stated. Their ethics do not permit "trick" or "catch" questions. Questions may have been tried out on sample groups, or subjected to statistical analysis, to determine their usefulness.

Written tests are often used in combination with performance tests, ratings of training and experience, and oral interviews. All of these measures combine to form the best-known means of finding the right person for the right job.

II. HOW TO PASS THE WRITTEN TEST

A. NATURE OF THE EXAMINATION

To prepare intelligently for civil service examinations, you should know how they differ from school examinations you have taken. In school you were assigned certain definite pages to read or subjects to cover. The examination questions were quite detailed and usually emphasized memory. Civil service exams, on the other hand, try to discover your present ability to perform the duties of a position, plus your potentiality to learn these duties. In other words, a civil service exam attempts to predict how successful you will be. Questions cover such a broad area that they cannot be as minute and detailed as school exam questions.

In the public service similar kinds of work, or positions, are grouped together in one "class." This process is known as *position-classification*. All the positions in a class are paid according to the salary range for that class. One class title covers all of these positions, and they are all tested by the same examination.

B. FOUR BASIC STEPS

1) Study the announcement

How, then, can you know what subjects to study? Our best answer is: "Learn as much as possible about the class of positions for which you've applied." The exam will test the knowledge, skills and abilities needed to do the work.

Your most valuable source of information about the position you want is the official exam announcement. This announcement lists the training and experience qualifications. Check these standards and apply only if you come reasonably close to meeting them.

The brief description of the position in the examination announcement offers some clues to the subjects which will be tested. Think about the job itself. Review the duties in your mind. Can you perform them, or are there some in which you are rusty? Fill in the blank spots in your preparation.

Many jurisdictions preview the written test in the exam announcement by including a section called "Knowledge and Abilities Required," "Scope of the Examination," or some similar heading. Here you will find out specifically what fields will be tested.

2) Review your own background

Once you learn in general what the position is all about, and what you need to know to do the work, ask yourself which subjects you already know fairly well and which need improvement. You may wonder whether to concentrate on improving your strong areas or on building some background in your fields of weakness. When the announcement has specified "some knowledge" or "considerable knowledge," or has used adjectives like "beginning principles of..." or "advanced ... methods," you can get a clue as to the number and difficulty of questions to be asked in any given field. More questions, and hence broader coverage, would be included for those subjects which are more important in the work. Now weigh your strengths and weaknesses against the job requirements and prepare accordingly.

3) Determine the level of the position

Another way to tell how intensively you should prepare is to understand the level of the job for which you are applying. Is it the entering level? In other words, is this the position in which beginners in a field of work are hired? Or is it an intermediate or advanced level? Sometimes this is indicated by such words as "Junior" or "Senior" in the class title. Other jurisdictions use Roman numerals to designate the level – Clerk I, Clerk II, for example. The word "Supervisor" sometimes appears in the title. If the level is not indicated by the title, check the description of duties. Will you be working under very close supervision, or will you have responsibility for independent decisions in this work?

4) Choose appropriate study materials

Now that you know the subjects to be examined and the relative amount of each subject to be covered, you can choose suitable study materials. For beginning level jobs, or even advanced ones, if you have a pronounced weakness in some aspect of your training, read a modern, standard textbook in that field. Be sure it is up to date and has general coverage. Such books are normally available at your library, and the librarian will be glad to help you locate one. For entry-level positions, questions of appropriate difficulty are chosen – neither highly advanced questions, nor those too simple. Such questions require careful thought but not advanced training.

If the position for which you are applying is technical or advanced, you will read more advanced, specialized material. If you are already familiar with the basic principles of your field, elementary textbooks would waste your time. Concentrate on advanced textbooks and technical periodicals. Think through the concepts and review difficult problems in your field.

These are all general sources. You can get more ideas on your own initiative, following these leads. For example, training manuals and publications of the government agency which employs workers in your field can be useful, particularly for technical and professional positions. A letter or visit to the government department involved may result in more specific study suggestions, and certainly will provide you with a more definite idea of the exact nature of the position you are seeking.

III. KINDS OF TESTS

Tests are used for purposes other than measuring knowledge and ability to perform specified duties. For some positions, it is equally important to test ability to make adjustments to new situations or to profit from training. In others, basic mental abilities not dependent on information are essential. Questions which test these things may not appear as pertinent to the duties of the position as those which test for knowledge and information. Yet they are often highly important parts of a fair examination. For very general questions, it is almost impossible to help you direct your study efforts. What we can do is to point out some of the more common of these general abilities needed in public service positions and describe some typical questions.

1) General information

Broad, general information has been found useful for predicting job success in some kinds of work. This is tested in a variety of ways, from vocabulary lists to questions about current events. Basic background in some field of work, such as sociology or economics, may be sampled in a group of questions. Often these are principles which have become familiar to most persons through exposure rather than through formal training. It is difficult to advise you how to study for these questions; being alert to the world around you is our best suggestion.

2) Verbal ability

An example of an ability needed in many positions is verbal or language ability. Verbal ability is, in brief, the ability to use and understand words. Vocabulary and grammar tests are typical measures of this ability. Reading comprehension or paragraph interpretation questions are common in many kinds of civil service tests. You are given a paragraph of written material and asked to find its central meaning.

3) Numerical ability
Number skills can be tested by the familiar arithmetic problem, by checking paired lists of numbers to see which are alike and which are different, or by interpreting charts and graphs. In the latter test, a graph may be printed in the test booklet which you are asked to use as the basis for answering questions.

4) Observation
A popular test for law-enforcement positions is the observation test. A picture is shown to you for several minutes, then taken away. Questions about the picture test your ability to observe both details and larger elements.

5) Following directions
In many positions in the public service, the employee must be able to carry out written instructions dependably and accurately. You may be given a chart with several columns, each column listing a variety of information. The questions require you to carry out directions involving the information given in the chart.

6) Skills and aptitudes
Performance tests effectively measure some manual skills and aptitudes. When the skill is one in which you are trained, such as typing or shorthand, you can practice. These tests are often very much like those given in business school or high school courses. For many of the other skills and aptitudes, however, no short-time preparation can be made. Skills and abilities natural to you or that you have developed throughout your lifetime are being tested.

Many of the general questions just described provide all the data needed to answer the questions and ask you to use your reasoning ability to find the answers. Your best preparation for these tests, as well as for tests of facts and ideas, is to be at your physical and mental best. You, no doubt, have your own methods of getting into an exam-taking mood and keeping "in shape." The next section lists some ideas on this subject.

IV. KINDS OF QUESTIONS

Only rarely is the "essay" question, which you answer in narrative form, used in civil service tests. Civil service tests are usually of the short-answer type. Full instructions for answering these questions will be given to you at the examination. But in case this is your first experience with short-answer questions and separate answer sheets, here is what you need to know:

1) **Multiple-choice Questions**
Most popular of the short-answer questions is the "multiple choice" or "best answer" question. It can be used, for example, to test for factual knowledge, ability to solve problems or judgment in meeting situations found at work.
A multiple-choice question is normally one of three types—
- It can begin with an incomplete statement followed by several possible endings. You are to find the one ending which *best* completes the statement, although some of the others may not be entirely wrong.
- It can also be a complete statement in the form of a question which is answered by choosing one of the statements listed.

- It can be in the form of a problem – again you select the best answer.

Here is an example of a multiple-choice question with a discussion which should give you some clues as to the method for choosing the right answer:

When an employee has a complaint about his assignment, the action which will *best* help him overcome his difficulty is to
    A. discuss his difficulty with his coworkers
    B. take the problem to the head of the organization
    C. take the problem to the person who gave him the assignment
    D. say nothing to anyone about his complaint

In answering this question, you should study each of the choices to find which is best. Consider choice "A" – Certainly an employee may discuss his complaint with fellow employees, but no change or improvement can result, and the complaint remains unresolved. Choice "B" is a poor choice since the head of the organization probably does not know what assignment you have been given, and taking your problem to him is known as "going over the head" of the supervisor. The supervisor, or person who made the assignment, is the person who can clarify it or correct any injustice. Choice "C" is, therefore, correct. To say nothing, as in choice "D," is unwise. Supervisors have and interest in knowing the problems employees are facing, and the employee is seeking a solution to his problem.

2) True/False Questions

The "true/false" or "right/wrong" form of question is sometimes used. Here a complete statement is given. Your job is to decide whether the statement is right or wrong.

SAMPLE: A roaming cell-phone call to a nearby city costs less than a non-roaming call to a distant city.

This statement is wrong, or false, since roaming calls are more expensive.

This is not a complete list of all possible question forms, although most of the others are variations of these common types. You will always get complete directions for answering questions. Be sure you understand *how* to mark your answers – ask questions until you do.

V. RECORDING YOUR ANSWERS

Computer terminals are used more and more today for many different kinds of exams.
For an examination with very few applicants, you may be told to record your answers in the test booklet itself. Separate answer sheets are much more common. If this separate answer sheet is to be scored by machine – and this is often the case – it is highly important that you mark your answers correctly in order to get credit.

An electronic scoring machine is often used in civil service offices because of the speed with which papers can be scored. Machine-scored answer sheets must be marked with a pencil, which will be given to you. This pencil has a high graphite content which responds to the electronic scoring machine. As a matter of fact, stray dots may register as answers, so do not let your pencil rest on the answer sheet while you are pondering the correct answer. Also, if your pencil lead breaks or is otherwise defective, ask for another.

Since the answer sheet will be dropped in a slot in the scoring machine, be careful not to bend the corners or get the paper crumpled.

The answer sheet normally has five vertical columns of numbers, with 30 numbers to a column. These numbers correspond to the question numbers in your test booklet. After each number, going across the page are four or five pairs of dotted lines. These short dotted lines have small letters or numbers above them. The first two pairs may also have a "T" or "F" above the letters. This indicates that the first two pairs only are to be used if the questions are of the true-false type. If the questions are multiple choice, disregard the "T" and "F" and pay attention only to the small letters or numbers.

Answer your questions in the manner of the sample that follows:

32. The largest city in the United States is
   A. Washington, D.C.
   B. New York City
   C. Chicago
   D. Detroit
   E. San Francisco

1) Choose the answer you think is best. (New York City is the largest, so "B" is correct.)
2) Find the row of dotted lines numbered the same as the question you are answering. (Find row number 32)
3) Find the pair of dotted lines corresponding to the answer. (Find the pair of lines under the mark "B.")
4) Make a solid black mark between the dotted lines.

VI. BEFORE THE TEST

Common sense will help you find procedures to follow to get ready for an examination. Too many of us, however, overlook these sensible measures. Indeed, nervousness and fatigue have been found to be the most serious reasons why applicants fail to do their best on civil service tests. Here is a list of reminders:

- Begin your preparation early – Don't wait until the last minute to go scurrying around for books and materials or to find out what the position is all about.
- Prepare continuously – An hour a night for a week is better than an all-night cram session. This has been definitely established. What is more, a night a week for a month will return better dividends than crowding your study into a shorter period of time.
- Locate the place of the exam – You have been sent a notice telling you when and where to report for the examination. If the location is in a different town or otherwise unfamiliar to you, it would be well to inquire the best route and learn something about the building.
- Relax the night before the test – Allow your mind to rest. Do not study at all that night. Plan some mild recreation or diversion; then go to bed early and get a good night's sleep.
- Get up early enough to make a leisurely trip to the place for the test – This way unforeseen events, traffic snarls, unfamiliar buildings, etc. will not upset you.
- Dress comfortably – A written test is not a fashion show. You will be known by number and not by name, so wear something comfortable.

- Leave excess paraphernalia at home – Shopping bags and odd bundles will get in your way. You need bring only the items mentioned in the official notice you received; usually everything you need is provided. Do not bring reference books to the exam. They will only confuse those last minutes and be taken away from you when in the test room.
- Arrive somewhat ahead of time – If because of transportation schedules you must get there very early, bring a newspaper or magazine to take your mind off yourself while waiting.
- Locate the examination room – When you have found the proper room, you will be directed to the seat or part of the room where you will sit. Sometimes you are given a sheet of instructions to read while you are waiting. Do not fill out any forms until you are told to do so; just read them and be prepared.
- Relax and prepare to listen to the instructions
- If you have any physical problem that may keep you from doing your best, be sure to tell the test administrator. If you are sick or in poor health, you really cannot do your best on the exam. You can come back and take the test some other time.

VII. AT THE TEST

The day of the test is here and you have the test booklet in your hand. The temptation to get going is very strong. Caution! There is more to success than knowing the right answers. You must know how to identify your papers and understand variations in the type of short-answer question used in this particular examination. Follow these suggestions for maximum results from your efforts:

1) Cooperate with the monitor

The test administrator has a duty to create a situation in which you can be as much at ease as possible. He will give instructions, tell you when to begin, check to see that you are marking your answer sheet correctly, and so on. He is not there to guard you, although he will see that your competitors do not take unfair advantage. He wants to help you do your best.

2) Listen to all instructions

Don't jump the gun! Wait until you understand all directions. In most civil service tests you get more time than you need to answer the questions. So don't be in a hurry. Read each word of instructions until you clearly understand the meaning. Study the examples, listen to all announcements and follow directions. Ask questions if you do not understand what to do.

3) Identify your papers

Civil service exams are usually identified by number only. You will be assigned a number; you must not put your name on your test papers. Be sure to copy your number correctly. Since more than one exam may be given, copy your exact examination title.

4) Plan your time

Unless you are told that a test is a "speed" or "rate of work" test, speed itself is usually not important. Time enough to answer all the questions will be provided, but this does not mean that you have all day. An overall time limit has been set. Divide the total time (in minutes) by the number of questions to determine the approximate time you have for each question.

5) Do not linger over difficult questions

If you come across a difficult question, mark it with a paper clip (useful to have along) and come back to it when you have been through the booklet. One caution if you do this – be sure to skip a number on your answer sheet as well. Check often to be sure that you have not lost your place and that you are marking in the row numbered the same as the question you are answering.

6) Read the questions

Be sure you know what the question asks! Many capable people are unsuccessful because they failed to *read* the questions correctly.

7) Answer all questions

Unless you have been instructed that a penalty will be deducted for incorrect answers, it is better to guess than to omit a question.

8) Speed tests

It is often better NOT to guess on speed tests. It has been found that on timed tests people are tempted to spend the last few seconds before time is called in marking answers at random – without even reading them – in the hope of picking up a few extra points. To discourage this practice, the instructions may warn you that your score will be "corrected" for guessing. That is, a penalty will be applied. The incorrect answers will be deducted from the correct ones, or some other penalty formula will be used.

9) Review your answers

If you finish before time is called, go back to the questions you guessed or omitted to give them further thought. Review other answers if you have time.

10) Return your test materials

If you are ready to leave before others have finished or time is called, take ALL your materials to the monitor and leave quietly. Never take any test material with you. The monitor can discover whose papers are not complete, and taking a test booklet may be grounds for disqualification.

VIII. EXAMINATION TECHNIQUES

1) Read the general instructions carefully. These are usually printed on the first page of the exam booklet. As a rule, these instructions refer to the timing of the examination; the fact that you should not start work until the signal and must stop work at a signal, etc. If there are any *special* instructions, such as a choice of questions to be answered, make sure that you note this instruction carefully.

2) When you are ready to start work on the examination, that is as soon as the signal has been given, read the instructions to each question booklet, underline any key words or phrases, such as *least, best, outline, describe* and the like. In this way you will tend to answer as requested rather than discover on reviewing your paper that you *listed without describing*, that you selected the *worst* choice rather than the *best* choice, etc.

3) If the examination is of the objective or multiple-choice type – that is, each question will also give a series of possible answers: A, B, C or D, and you are called upon to select the best answer and write the letter next to that answer on your answer paper – it is advisable to start answering each question in turn. There may be anywhere from 50 to 100 such questions in the three or four hours allotted and you can see how much time would be taken if you read through all the questions before beginning to answer any. Furthermore, if you come across a question or group of questions which you know would be difficult to answer, it would undoubtedly affect your handling of all the other questions.

4) If the examination is of the essay type and contains but a few questions, it is a moot point as to whether you should read all the questions before starting to answer any one. Of course, if you are given a choice – say five out of seven and the like – then it is essential to read all the questions so you can eliminate the two that are most difficult. If, however, you are asked to answer all the questions, there may be danger in trying to answer the easiest one first because you may find that you will spend too much time on it. The best technique is to answer the first question, then proceed to the second, etc.

5) Time your answers. Before the exam begins, write down the time it started, then add the time allowed for the examination and write down the time it must be completed, then divide the time available somewhat as follows:
   - If 3-1/2 hours are allowed, that would be 210 minutes. If you have 80 objective-type questions, that would be an average of 2-1/2 minutes per question. Allow yourself no more than 2 minutes per question, or a total of 160 minutes, which will permit about 50 minutes to review.
   - If for the time allotment of 210 minutes there are 7 essay questions to answer, that would average about 30 minutes a question. Give yourself only 25 minutes per question so that you have about 35 minutes to review.

6) The most important instruction is to *read each question* and make sure you know what is wanted. The second most important instruction is to *time yourself properly* so that you answer every question. The third most important instruction is to *answer every question*. Guess if you have to but include something for each question. Remember that you will receive no credit for a blank and will probably receive some credit if you write something in answer to an essay question. If you guess a letter – say "B" for a multiple-choice question – you may have guessed right. If you leave a blank as an answer to a multiple-choice question, the examiners may respect your feelings but it will not add a point to your score. Some exams may penalize you for wrong answers, so in such cases *only*, you may not want to guess unless you have some basis for your answer.

7) Suggestions
   a. Objective-type questions
      1. Examine the question booklet for proper sequence of pages and questions
      2. Read all instructions carefully
      3. Skip any question which seems too difficult; return to it after all other questions have been answered
      4. Apportion your time properly; do not spend too much time on any single question or group of questions

     5. Note and underline key words – *all, most, fewest, least, best, worst, same, opposite,* etc.
     6. Pay particular attention to negatives
     7. Note unusual option, e.g., unduly long, short, complex, different or similar in content to the body of the question
     8. Observe the use of "hedging" words – *probably, may, most likely,* etc.
     9. Make sure that your answer is put next to the same number as the question
    10. Do not second-guess unless you have good reason to believe the second answer is definitely more correct
    11. Cross out original answer if you decide another answer is more accurate; do not erase until you are ready to hand your paper in
    12. Answer all questions; guess unless instructed otherwise
    13. Leave time for review

  b. Essay questions
    1. Read each question carefully
    2. Determine exactly what is wanted. Underline key words or phrases.
    3. Decide on outline or paragraph answer
    4. Include many different points and elements unless asked to develop any one or two points or elements
    5. Show impartiality by giving pros and cons unless directed to select one side only
    6. Make and write down any assumptions you find necessary to answer the questions
    7. Watch your English, grammar, punctuation and choice of words
    8. Time your answers; don't crowd material

8) Answering the essay question

Most essay questions can be answered by framing the specific response around several key words or ideas. Here are a few such key words or ideas:

M's: manpower, materials, methods, money, management
P's: purpose, program, policy, plan, procedure, practice, problems, pitfalls, personnel, public relations

  a. Six basic steps in handling problems:
    1. Preliminary plan and background development
    2. Collect information, data and facts
    3. Analyze and interpret information, data and facts
    4. Analyze and develop solutions as well as make recommendations
    5. Prepare report and sell recommendations
    6. Install recommendations and follow up effectiveness

  b. Pitfalls to avoid
    1. *Taking things for granted* – A statement of the situation does not necessarily imply that each of the elements is necessarily true; for example, a complaint may be invalid and biased so that all that can be taken for granted is that a complaint has been registered

2. *Considering only one side of a situation* – Wherever possible, indicate several alternatives and then point out the reasons you selected the best one
3. *Failing to indicate follow up* – Whenever your answer indicates action on your part, make certain that you will take proper follow-up action to see how successful your recommendations, procedures or actions turn out to be
4. *Taking too long in answering any single question* – Remember to time your answers properly

IX. AFTER THE TEST

Scoring procedures differ in detail among civil service jurisdictions although the general principles are the same. Whether the papers are hand-scored or graded by machine we have described, they are nearly always graded by number. That is, the person who marks the paper knows only the number – never the name – of the applicant. Not until all the papers have been graded will they be matched with names. If other tests, such as training and experience or oral interview ratings have been given, scores will be combined. Different parts of the examination usually have different weights. For example, the written test might count 60 percent of the final grade, and a rating of training and experience 40 percent. In many jurisdictions, veterans will have a certain number of points added to their grades.

After the final grade has been determined, the names are placed in grade order and an eligible list is established. There are various methods for resolving ties between those who get the same final grade – probably the most common is to place first the name of the person whose application was received first. Job offers are made from the eligible list in the order the names appear on it. You will be notified of your grade and your rank as soon as all these computations have been made. This will be done as rapidly as possible.

People who are found to meet the requirements in the announcement are called "eligibles." Their names are put on a list of eligible candidates. An eligible's chances of getting a job depend on how high he stands on this list and how fast agencies are filling jobs from the list.

When a job is to be filled from a list of eligibles, the agency asks for the names of people on the list of eligibles for that job. When the civil service commission receives this request, it sends to the agency the names of the three people highest on this list. Or, if the job to be filled has specialized requirements, the office sends the agency the names of the top three persons who meet these requirements from the general list.

The appointing officer makes a choice from among the three people whose names were sent to him. If the selected person accepts the appointment, the names of the others are put back on the list to be considered for future openings.

That is the rule in hiring from all kinds of eligible lists, whether they are for typist, carpenter, chemist, or something else. For every vacancy, the appointing officer has his choice of any one of the top three eligibles on the list. This explains why the person whose name is on top of the list sometimes does not get an appointment when some of the persons lower on the list do. If the appointing officer chooses the second or third eligible, the No. 1 eligible does not get a job at once, but stays on the list until he is appointed or the list is terminated.

X. HOW TO PASS THE INTERVIEW TEST

The examination for which you applied requires an oral interview test. You have already taken the written test and you are now being called for the interview test – the final part of the formal examination.

You may think that it is not possible to prepare for an interview test and that there are no procedures to follow during an interview. Our purpose is to point out some things you can do in advance that will help you and some good rules to follow and pitfalls to avoid while you are being interviewed.

What is an interview supposed to test?

The written examination is designed to test the technical knowledge and competence of the candidate; the oral is designed to evaluate intangible qualities, not readily measured otherwise, and to establish a list showing the relative fitness of each candidate – as measured against his competitors – for the position sought. Scoring is not on the basis of "right" and "wrong," but on a sliding scale of values ranging from "not passable" to "outstanding." As a matter of fact, it is possible to achieve a relatively low score without a single "incorrect" answer because of evident weakness in the qualities being measured.

Occasionally, an examination may consist entirely of an oral test – either an individual or a group oral. In such cases, information is sought concerning the technical knowledges and abilities of the candidate, since there has been no written examination for this purpose. More commonly, however, an oral test is used to supplement a written examination.

Who conducts interviews?

The composition of oral boards varies among different jurisdictions. In nearly all, a representative of the personnel department serves as chairman. One of the members of the board may be a representative of the department in which the candidate would work. In some cases, "outside experts" are used, and, frequently, a businessman or some other representative of the general public is asked to serve. Labor and management or other special groups may be represented. The aim is to secure the services of experts in the appropriate field.

However the board is composed, it is a good idea (and not at all improper or unethical) to ascertain in advance of the interview who the members are and what groups they represent. When you are introduced to them, you will have some idea of their backgrounds and interests, and at least you will not stutter and stammer over their names.

What should be done before the interview?

While knowledge about the board members is useful and takes some of the surprise element out of the interview, there is other preparation which is more substantive. It *is* possible to prepare for an oral interview – in several ways:

1) Keep a copy of your application and review it carefully before the interview

This may be the only document before the oral board, and the starting point of the interview. Know what education and experience you have listed there, and the sequence and dates of all of it. Sometimes the board will ask you to review the highlights of your experience for them; you should not have to hem and haw doing it.

2) Study the class specification and the examination announcement

Usually, the oral board has one or both of these to guide them. The qualities, characteristics or knowledges required by the position sought are stated in these documents. They offer valuable clues as to the nature of the oral interview. For example, if the job involves supervisory responsibilities, the announcement will usually indicate that knowledge of modern supervisory methods and the qualifications of the candidate as a supervisor will be tested. If so, you can expect such questions, frequently in the form of a hypothetical situation which you are expected to solve. NEVER go into an oral without knowledge of the duties and responsibilities of the job you seek.

3) Think through each qualification required

Try to visualize the kind of questions you would ask if you were a board member. How well could you answer them? Try especially to appraise your own knowledge and background in each area, *measured against the job sought*, and identify any areas in which you are weak. Be critical and realistic – do not flatter yourself.

4) Do some general reading in areas in which you feel you may be weak

For example, if the job involves supervision and your past experience has NOT, some general reading in supervisory methods and practices, particularly in the field of human relations, might be useful. Do NOT study agency procedures or detailed manuals. The oral board will be testing your understanding and capacity, not your memory.

5) Get a good night's sleep and watch your general health and mental attitude

You will want a clear head at the interview. Take care of a cold or any other minor ailment, and of course, no hangovers.

What should be done on the day of the interview?

Now comes the day of the interview itself. Give yourself plenty of time to get there. Plan to arrive somewhat ahead of the scheduled time, particularly if your appointment is in the fore part of the day. If a previous candidate fails to appear, the board might be ready for you a bit early. By early afternoon an oral board is almost invariably behind schedule if there are many candidates, and you may have to wait. Take along a book or magazine to read, or your application to review, but leave any extraneous material in the waiting room when you go in for your interview. In any event, relax and compose yourself.

The matter of dress is important. The board is forming impressions about you – from your experience, your manners, your attitude, and your appearance. Give your personal appearance careful attention. Dress your best, but not your flashiest. Choose conservative, appropriate clothing, and be sure it is immaculate. This is a business interview, and your appearance should indicate that you regard it as such. Besides, being well groomed and properly dressed will help boost your confidence.

Sooner or later, someone will call your name and escort you into the interview room. *This is it.* From here on you are on your own. It is too late for any more preparation. But remember, you asked for this opportunity to prove your fitness, and you are here because your request was granted.

What happens when you go in?

The usual sequence of events will be as follows: The clerk (who is often the board stenographer) will introduce you to the chairman of the oral board, who will introduce you to the other members of the board. Acknowledge the introductions before you sit down. Do not be surprised if you find a microphone facing you or a stenotypist sitting by. Oral interviews are usually recorded in the event of an appeal or other review.

Usually the chairman of the board will open the interview by reviewing the highlights of your education and work experience from your application – primarily for the benefit of the other members of the board, as well as to get the material into the record. Do not interrupt or comment unless there is an error or significant misinterpretation; if that is the case, do not hesitate. But do not quibble about insignificant matters. Also, he will usually ask you some question about your education, experience or your present job – partly to get you to start talking and to establish the interviewing "rapport." He may start the actual questioning, or turn it over to one of the other members. Frequently, each member undertakes the questioning on a particular area, one in which he is perhaps most competent, so you can expect each member to participate in the examination. Because time is limited, you may also expect some rather abrupt switches in the direction the questioning takes, so do not be upset by it. Normally, a board member will not pursue a single line of questioning unless he discovers a particular strength or weakness.

After each member has participated, the chairman will usually ask whether any member has any further questions, then will ask you if you have anything you wish to add. Unless you are expecting this question, it may floor you. Worse, it may start you off on an extended, extemporaneous speech. The board is not usually seeking more information. The question is principally to offer you a last opportunity to present further qualifications or to indicate that you have nothing to add. So, if you feel that a significant qualification or characteristic has been overlooked, it is proper to point it out in a sentence or so. Do not compliment the board on the thoroughness of their examination – they have been sketchy, and you know it. If you wish, merely say, "No thank you, I have nothing further to add." This is a point where you can "talk yourself out" of a good impression or fail to present an important bit of information. Remember, *you close the interview yourself*.

The chairman will then say, "That is all, Mr. _____, thank you." Do not be startled; the interview is over, and quicker than you think. Thank him, gather your belongings and take your leave. Save your sigh of relief for the other side of the door.

How to put your best foot forward

Throughout this entire process, you may feel that the board individually and collectively is trying to pierce your defenses, seek out your hidden weaknesses and embarrass and confuse you. Actually, this is not true. They are obliged to make an appraisal of your qualifications for the job you are seeking, and they want to see you in your best light. Remember, they must interview all candidates and a non-cooperative candidate may become a failure in spite of their best efforts to bring out his qualifications. Here are 15 suggestions that will help you:

1) Be natural – Keep your attitude confident, not cocky

If you are not confident that you can do the job, do not expect the board to be. Do not apologize for your weaknesses, try to bring out your strong points. The board is interested in a positive, not negative, presentation. Cockiness will antagonize any board member and make him wonder if you are covering up a weakness by a false show of strength.

2) Get comfortable, but don't lounge or sprawl

Sit erectly but not stiffly. A careless posture may lead the board to conclude that you are careless in other things, or at least that you are not impressed by the importance of the occasion. Either conclusion is natural, even if incorrect. Do not fuss with your clothing, a pencil or an ashtray. Your hands may occasionally be useful to emphasize a point; do not let them become a point of distraction.

3) Do not wisecrack or make small talk

This is a serious situation, and your attitude should show that you consider it as such. Further, the time of the board is limited – they do not want to waste it, and neither should you.

4) Do not exaggerate your experience or abilities

In the first place, from information in the application or other interviews and sources, the board may know more about you than you think. Secondly, you probably will not get away with it. An experienced board is rather adept at spotting such a situation, so do not take the chance.

5) If you know a board member, do not make a point of it, yet do not hide it

Certainly you are not fooling him, and probably not the other members of the board. Do not try to take advantage of your acquaintanceship – it will probably do you little good.

6) Do not dominate the interview

Let the board do that. They will give you the clues – do not assume that you have to do all the talking. Realize that the board has a number of questions to ask you, and do not try to take up all the interview time by showing off your extensive knowledge of the answer to the first one.

7) Be attentive

You only have 20 minutes or so, and you should keep your attention at its sharpest throughout. When a member is addressing a problem or question to you, give him your undivided attention. Address your reply principally to him, but do not exclude the other board members.

8) Do not interrupt

A board member may be stating a problem for you to analyze. He will ask you a question when the time comes. Let him state the problem, and wait for the question.

9) Make sure you understand the question

Do not try to answer until you are sure what the question is. If it is not clear, restate it in your own words or ask the board member to clarify it for you. However, do not haggle about minor elements.

10) Reply promptly but not hastily

A common entry on oral board rating sheets is "candidate responded readily," or "candidate hesitated in replies." Respond as promptly and quickly as you can, but do not jump to a hasty, ill-considered answer.

11) Do not be peremptory in your answers

A brief answer is proper – but do not fire your answer back. That is a losing game from your point of view. The board member can probably ask questions much faster than you can answer them.

12) Do not try to create the answer you think the board member wants

He is interested in what kind of mind you have and how it works – not in playing games. Furthermore, he can usually spot this practice and will actually grade you down on it.

13) Do not switch sides in your reply merely to agree with a board member

Frequently, a member will take a contrary position merely to draw you out and to see if you are willing and able to defend your point of view. Do not start a debate, yet do not surrender a good position. If a position is worth taking, it is worth defending.

14) Do not be afraid to admit an error in judgment if you are shown to be wrong

The board knows that you are forced to reply without any opportunity for careful consideration. Your answer may be demonstrably wrong. If so, admit it and get on with the interview.

15) Do not dwell at length on your present job

The opening question may relate to your present assignment. Answer the question but do not go into an extended discussion. You are being examined for a *new* job, not your present one. As a matter of fact, try to phrase ALL your answers in terms of the job for which you are being examined.

Basis of Rating

Probably you will forget most of these "do's" and "don'ts" when you walk into the oral interview room. Even remembering them all will not ensure you a passing grade. Perhaps you did not have the qualifications in the first place. But remembering them will help you to put your best foot forward, without treading on the toes of the board members.

Rumor and popular opinion to the contrary notwithstanding, an oral board wants you to make the best appearance possible. They know you are under pressure – but they also want to see how you respond to it as a guide to what your reaction would be under the pressures of the job you seek. They will be influenced by the degree of poise you display, the personal traits you show and the manner in which you respond.

ABOUT THIS BOOK

This book contains tests divided into Examination Sections. Go through each test, answering every question in the margin. We have also attached a sample answer sheet at the back of the book that can be removed and used. At the end of each test look at the answer key and check your answers. On the ones you got wrong, look at the right answer choice and learn. Do not fill in the answers first. Do not memorize the questions and answers, but understand the answer and principles involved. On your test, the questions will likely be different from the samples. Questions are changed and new ones added. If you understand these past questions you should have success with any changes that arise. Tests may consist of several types of questions. We have additional books on each subject should more study be advisable or necessary for you. Finally, the more you study, the better prepared you will be. This book is intended to be the last thing you study before you walk into the examination room. Prior study of relevant texts is also recommended. NLC publishes some of these in our Fundamental Series. Knowledge and good sense are important factors in passing your exam. Good luck also helps. So now study this Passbook, absorb the material contained within and take that knowledge into the examination. Then do your best to pass that exam.

EXAMINATION SECTION

EXAMINATION SECTION
TEST 1

DIRECTIONS: Each question or incomplete statement is followed by several suggested answers or completions. Select the one that BEST answers the question or completes the statement. *PRINT THE LETTER OF THE CORRECT ANSWER IN THE SPACE AT THE RIGHT.*

1. During an interview with a witness, the investigator should carefully observe the witness's gestures and facial expressions.
   To interpret the meaning of these actions, the investigator should do all of the following EXCEPT to

   A. try to *read* the situation in which a puzzling gesture is used
   B. ask questions that relate specifically to the gesture
   C. take an educated guess based on past experience
   D. rely on the standard meaning of the gesture

   1.____

2. Of the following, the MOST important skill for a supervisor of investigators to possess is the ability to

   A. communicate effectively
   B. obtain the respect of his staff
   C. remain calm in pressure situations
   D. develop high morale among his subordinates

   2.____

3. Following are three statements concerning the preparation by an investigator of a written statement taken from a witness:
   I. Have each page initialed by the witness
   II. Correct and initial any mistakes in grammar that are made by the witness
   III. Leave space between paragraphs to facilitate the addition of notes and comments.

   Which of the following correctly classifies the above statements into those that are valid and those that are not?

   A. I is valid, but II and III are not.
   B. II and III are valid, but I is not.
   C. III is valid, but I and II are not.
   D. I and II are valid, but III is not.

   3.____

4. Assume, as an investigator, you are questioning an employee of your agency suspected of misstating previous work experience on his employment application. You notice that the employee is reluctant to admit that his previous statements were inaccurate.
   The one of the following that is the BEST method of obtaining the truth from this employee would be for you to

   A. tell him that his job is not in jeopardy
   B. make him feel he is not being criticized
   C. have him discuss the matter with your supervisor
   D. allow him to correct any inaccuracies on his employment application

   4.____

5. If several witnesses describing the same occurrence agree on most details, the investigator should then

   A. determine whether or not these witnesses were in communication with each other
   B. assume that such agreement means that the recollection was correct
   C. assume that the witnesses' observations were incorrect since two or more people usually will not agree on the same details
   D. question the witnesses again, concentrating on the details on which they differ

6. In trying to obtain a statement from a hospitalized individual who is unable to receive visitors, it would be BEST for an investigator

   A. draw up a statement from his own knowledge of the case and ask a hospital staff member to have the patient sign the statement when he is well
   B. contact the patient's family and arrange for an appointment to see the patient as soon as his condition permits
   C. leave a message at the hospital for the patient to contact him when he is available to receive visitors
   D. appear at the hospital with proper identification and request official permission from the hospital administrator to speak with the patient

7. Among employment specialists, it is generally agreed that the value of character references on employment applications is

   A. *limited,* chiefly because such references are written only by personal friends of the applicant
   B. *significant,* chiefly because information they transmit is unavailable from other sources
   C. *limited,* chiefly because they tend to give only favorable information
   D. *significant,* chiefly because they have direct knowledge of the applicant's abilities

8. The MOST important requirement of a person who is testifying about a criminal act that he witnessed is that he

   A. was conscious and attentive during the crime
   B. is a respected and trustworthy member of the community
   C. is without a prior criminal record
   D. gives a consistent account of the details of the crime

9. Assume that, after taking a written statement from Employee A, an investigator is about to obtain his signature. He wants to ask Employee B, a co-worker, to witness the signing but Employee B is not available at that time.
   To expedite the investigation, it would be MOST desirable for the investigator to

   A. have Employee A sign the statement and obtain Employee B's signature at a later time
   B. ask an available disinterested party to witness Employee A's signature
   C. witness Employee A's signature himself
   D. have Employee A sign when Employee B is available

10. Witnesses are usually MOST willing to discuss an event when they are 10.____

    A. disinterested in the subsequent investigation
    B. interviewed immediately following the event
    C. interviewed for the first time
    D. known by the investigator

11. To determine the former addresses of a person who has moved several times within the same locality, it would be BEST to contact 11.____

    A. the Post Office   B. insurance companies
    C. public utilities   D. banking institutions

12. The one of the following that is CHARACTERISTIC of the interview as compared with the observation approach to investigation is that an interview generally 12.____

    A. requires more time to complete adequately
    B. is more likely to result in incomplete information
    C. is less applicable to the study of an individual's beliefs and values
    D. is less costly to conduct

13. The use of slang on the part of an investigator when questioning subjects is generally 13.____

    A. *inadvisable*; chiefly because it leads to misinterpretations
    B. *advisable*; chiefly because it will insure objective responses
    C. *inadvisable*; chiefly because it can compromise the investigator's dignity
    D. *advisable*; chiefly because it can promote ease of speech and understanding

14. Assume that a job applicant claims on his employment application that he has just recently become a United States citizen.
    Of the following, it would be MOST appropriate for you, in verifying this matter, to consult the 14.____

    A. Department of State   B. Treasury Department
    C. Immigration and Naturalization Service D. Department of Justice

15. If an investigator receives an anonymous phone call from a person claiming to have knowledge of criminal behavior in an agency which is currently being investigated, the investigator should 15.____

    A. listen politely and make notes on the important facts given by the informant
    B. tell the informant what has already been discovered and ask if he has anything to add
    C. question the informant to obtain all the information he has
    D. ask the informant to submit his information in writing

16. When interviewing a child, an investigator should keep in mind the fact that children 16.____

    A. are psychologically incapable of giving an accurate statement
    B. usually have faulty perception
    C. are easily led into making incorrect statements since they tend to agree with the questioner
    D. will often make statements which are pure fantasy because they are not as observant as adults

17. Following are three statements concerning the use of an investigator's notebook in court:
   I. A looseleaf-type notebook creates a more favorable impression in the courtroom than a bound notebook because the former permits the removal of pages unrelated to the case in question
   II. An investigator's notebook should be written in ink, not pencil, because of the need for permanence
   III. The notebook should ideally contain the notes of only one investigation so that its scrutiny will not involve the disclosure of information relating to other investigations

   Which of the following CORRECTLY classifies the above statements into those which are valid and those which are not valid?

   A. I and III are valid, but II is not.
   B. I and II are valid, but III is not.
   C. I is valid, but II and III are not.
   D. II and III are valid, but I is not.

18. The first three digits of a social security number are coded for the

   A. age of the cardholder when the card was issued
   B. cardholder's initials
   C. year the card was issued
   D. area in which the card was issued

19. Two methods of obtaining personal background information are the personal interview and the telephone inquiry.
   As compared with the latter, the personal type of interview USUALLY _____ flexibility in questioning _____ frankness.

   A. permits; but discourages
   B. restricts; but encourages
   C. permits; and encourages
   D. restricts; and discourages

20. One of the important functions of investigators is to perform surveillances without the knowledge of the subject. If a subject thinks he is being followed, he is LEAST likely to react by

   A. reversing his course to see whether anyone else does likewise
   B. boarding a subway car and getting off just before it pulls out
   C. attempting to pass the surveillant several times to view him face-to-face
   D. using the services of a *convoy* to observe whether he is being followed

21. Assume that you are conducting an interview with a prospective employee who is of limited mental ability and low socio-economic status.
   Of the following, it is MOST likely that asking him many open-ended questions about his work experience would cause him to respond

   A. articulately   B. reluctantly
   C. comfortably   D. aggressively

22. Assume, as an investigator, you want a witness to sign a statement. 22.____
Which of the following phrases is MOST likely to secure his signature?

   A. I would appreciate it if you would sign the statement at this time.
   B. Sign the statement where indicated.
   C. Sign the statement when you get the chance.
   D. If the statement is generally correct, please sign it.

23. During an interview, a subject makes statements an investigator knows to be false. 23.____
Of the following, it would be MOST appropriate for the investigator to

   A. point out each inconsistency in the subject's story as soon as the investigator detects it
   B. interrupt the subject and request that he submit to a polygraph test
   C. allow the subject to continue talking until he becomes enmeshed in his lies and then confront him with his falsehoods
   D. allow the subject to finish what he has to say and then explicitly inform him that it is a crime to lie to a government employee

24. One of the major objectives of a pre-employment interview is to get the interviewee to 24.____
respond freely to inquiries. The one of the following actions that would be MOST likely to restrict the conversation of the interviewee would be for the investigator to

   A. keep a stenographic record of the interviewee's statements
   B. ask questions requiring complete explanations
   C. pose direct, specific questions to the interviewee
   D. allow the interviewee to respond to questions at his own pace

25. A list of the names, addresses, and titles of city employees is made available to the public by the 25.____

   A. civil service commission
   B. comptroller's office
   C. mayor's office
   D. municipal reference and research center

KEY (CORRECT ANSWERS)

1. D
2. A
3. A
4. B
5. A

6. B
7. C
8. A
9. B
10. B

11. C
12. D
13. D
14. C
15. C

16. C
17. D
18. D
19. C
20. C

21. B
22. B
23. C
24. A
25. D

EXAMINATION SECTION
TEST 1

DIRECTIONS: Each question or incomplete statement is followed by several suggested answers or completions. Select the one that BEST answers the question or completes the statement. *PRINT THE LETTER OF THE CORRECT ANSWER IN THE SPACE AT THE RIGHT.*

1. Assume you are supervising a group of investigators. Your unit is assigned a rush job requiring a special skill and overtime work.
   Of the following, the MOST appropriate method of choosing the investigator to do this job is to

   A. assign the investigator who has the special skill required for the job
   B. ask an investigator who has previously indicated a willingness to work overtime
   C. call for a volunteer to perform this work
   D. offer the job to the investigator who is next in line to work overtime

2. Formal training programs can help remedy specific problems in an investigative unit. The one of the following that is NOT an intended result of such training programs is to

   A. eliminate the need for on-the-job training for new investigators
   B. help reduce the amount of overtime paid
   C. minimize the number of grievances made by investigators
   D. develop a pool of trained investigators needed for agency expansion

3. Periodic evaluation of subordinates' performance on the job serves all of the following purposes EXCEPT to

   A. point out weaknesses in performance to subordinates so that attempts can be made to eliminate them
   B. identify capable subordinates and insure that they are promoted
   C. indicate those subordinates who deserve training for greater responsibilities
   D. identify those subordinates who have exceptional ability

4. All of the following are proper objectives in the investigation of outside complaints about agency personnel EXCEPT the protection of the

   A. integrity and reputation of the staff
   B. public interest in identifying wrongdoers
   C. organization from liability resulting from unjust claims
   D. accused employees from disciplinary action

5. Assume that one of your subordinates had had a minor accident while performing a surveillance. In spite of your repeated demands, the subordinate refuses to prepare an accident report because he was only slightly injured. Of the following actions, it would be BEST in this situation for you to

   A. contact your superior to discuss disciplinary action
   B. have the employee file an affidavit absolving you of any responsibility for his injury
   C. ask the employee to submit a doctor's note to you on the extent of his injury
   D. call a meeting of subordinate personnel to discuss this situation

6. The one of the following that is likely to provide subordinates with the GREATEST satisfaction on the job is

    A. compensation for overtime production
    B. challenging and interesting work
    C. compensation proportional to the amount of work produced
    D. minimum responsibility for the completion of work

7. An employee is GENERALLY considered guilty of insubordination when he

    A. refuses to obey a supervisor's order with which he disagrees
    B. declines to carry out a directive he genuinely believes will cause him personal injury
    C. uses foul or abusive language among other work group members
    D. reports to work late after being warned not do do so

8. The one of the following that is GENERALLY characteristic of the more effective supervisors is that they

    A. specify every detail of the work to be done
    B. give subordinates leeway in the methods they use to complete their work
    C. supervise more closely than the less effective supervisors
    D. tend to be production-centered rather than employee-centered

9. If workers participate in planning, making important decisions, and the like, the supervisor will lose prestige and his authority will deteriorate.
    This statement is

    A. *true* because people have little respect for a leader who seeks their advice
    B. *true* because a supervisor must establish a firm command over his subordinates to be effective
    C. *false* because a skillful supervisor works with his subordinates to establish a goal and then works to reach it
    D. *false* because a supervisor gains prestige only by making all important decisions himself

10. As a supervisor, you note that while one of your subordinates does what he is told to do, he seems disinterested and lacks motivation in performing his work.
    Of the following, the BEST action for you to take to motivate this employee would be to

    A. transfer him to a more active unit
    B. give him less desirable work
    C. give him more responsibility
    D. assign him to work with a more experienced employee

11. Newly appointed supervisors will often assume responsibility for work which could be handled by their subordinates.
    Of the following, the MOST likely result of such a practice would be that the

    A. supervisor will gain the confidence of his subordinates
    B. subordinates' sense of initiative and responsibility will diminish
    C. supervisor will note an increase in the job satisfaction of his subordinates
    D. subordinates will have more time to learn more complex job skills

12. In order to accomplish the work of his unit MOST effectively, a supervisor of investigators should

    A. do the important work himself
    B. assign complete responsibility for the completion of work only to his more productive subordinates
    C. judiciously delegate authority to make decisions to his subordinates
    D. give sensitive and responsible work only to his most competent investigators

13. Assume, as a supervisor, you are approached by one of the investigators in your unit with what you consider to be a minor grievance.
    Of the following, the BEST way to handle this situation is to

    A. postpone taking any action since the passage of time usually resolves minor grievances
    B. try to resolve the problem immediately before it gets out of hand
    C. tell the investigator not to be concerned with minor grievances
    D. thank the investigator for calling the grievance to your attention and await further developments

14. Following are three guidelines a supervisor might follow in handling criticism by a superior:
    I. Consider the source of criticism before taking any action.
    II. Try to react calmly to criticism that is not justified.
    III. Analyze carefully only the criticism that requires a response.
    Which of the following CORRECTLY classifies the above guidelines into those which are valid and those which are not valid?

    A. I is valid, but II and III are not.
    B. I and II are valid, but III is not.
    C. II and III are valid, but I is not.
    D. III is valid, but I and III are not.

15. Assume that a supervisor notices that several of his subordinates, who are normally punctual, have been late for work quite often during the last few months.
    Which one of the following actions should the supervisor take FIRST in dealing with this problem?

    A. Refer the matter to the personnel staff of his agency.
    B. Schedule counseling sessions on the need for being prompt.
    C. Review his own supervision to determine whether it has been adequate.
    D. Inform the subordinates that exact records of their latenesses are being kept.

16. Following are three statements concerning principles of delegation:
    I. Supervisors should not be held accountable for work that has been delegated to their subordinates.
    II. Subordinates should normally have only one line supervisor.
    III. When subordinates are given authority that is limited by factors such as departmental rules, their responsibility is also limited.
    Which of the following BEST classifies the above statements into those that are valid and those that are not valid?

A. I is valid, but II and III are not.
B. II is valid, but I and III are not.
C. I and II are valid, but III is not.
D. II and III are valid, but I is not.

17. Following are six steps that should be taken in the course of report preparation:
    I. Outlining the material for presentation in the report.
    II. Analyzing and interpreting the facts
    III. Analyzing the problem
    IV. Reaching conclusions
    V. Writing, revising, and rewriting the final copy
    VI. Collecting data

    According to the principles of good report writing, the CORRECT order in which these steps should be taken is

    A. VI, III, II, I, IV, V
    B. III, VI, II, IV, I, V
    C. III, VI, II, I, IV, V
    D. VI, II, III, IV, I, V

18. Following are three statements concerning written reports:
    I. Clarity is generally more essential in oral reports than in written reports.
    II. Short sentences composed of simple words are generally preferred to complex sentences and difficult words.
    III. Abbreviations may be used whenever they are customary and will not distract the attention of the reader.

    Which of the following choices CORRECTLY classifies the above statements into those which are valid and those which are not valid?

    A. I and II are valid, but III is not valid.
    B. I is valid, but II and III are not valid.
    C. II and III are valid, but I is not valid.
    D. III is valid, but I and II are not valid.

19. In order to produce a report written in a style that is both understandable and effective, an investigator should apply the principles of unity, coherence, and emphasis. The one of the following which is the BEST example of the principle of coherence is

    A. interlinking sentences so that thoughts flow smoothly
    B. having each sentence express a single idea to facilitate comprehension
    C. arranging important points in prominent positions so they are not overlooked
    D. developing the main idea fully to insure complete consideration

20. Following are three statements concerning public relations in a city agency:
    I. Public relations in an agency should be the sole responsibility of a trained public relations professional
    II. Public relations involves every contact the agency has with the public, whether the contact is in person or by letter or telephone
    III. The public should be told by the agency what it is going to do and how it is going to do it before hearing a version from other sources which may be distorted

    Which of the following choices CORRECTLY classifies the above statements into those which are correct and those which are not?

A. I and II are correct, but III is not.
B. I is correct, but II and III are not.
C. II is correct, but I and III are not.
D. II and III are correct, but I is not.

21. Communication, both written and oral, is essential to the functioning of any organization. Written communication is generally more appropriate than oral communication when the information being transmitted   21.____

    A. concerns a small group of people
    B. has long-term significance
    C. is only of minimal importance
    D. is concise and simple to comprehend

22. Subordinates are MOST likely to accept changes in their work plans and schedules when their supervisor   22.____

    A. advises them that such changes must be implemented because they have been ordered by management
    B. gives them some background to help them understand the need for the changes
    C. tells them that even though he disagrees with the changes, they must be adhered to
    D. informs them he will follow up to determine how effective such changes are

Questions 23-25.

DIRECTIONS: Below is a report consisting of 15 numbered sentences, some of which are not consistent with the principles of good report writing. Questions 23 through 25 are to be answered SOLELY on the basis of the information contained in the report and your knowledge of investigative principles and practices.

To: Tom Smith, Administrative Investigator
From: John Jones, Senior Investigator
1. On January 7, I received a call from Mrs. H. Harris of 684 Sunset Street, Brooklyn.
2. Mrs. Harris informed me that she wanted to report an instance of fraud relating to public assistance payments being received by her neighbor, Mrs. I. Wallace.
3. I advised her that such a subject would best be discussed in person.
4. I then arranged a field visitation for January 10 at Mrs. Harris' apartment, 684 Sunset Street, Brooklyn.
5. On January 10, I discussed the basis for Mrs. Harris' charge against Mrs. Wallace at the former's apartment.
6. She stated that her neighbor is receiving Aid to Dependent Children payments for seven children, but that only three of her children are still living with her.
7. In addition, Mrs. Harris also claimed that her husband, whom she reported to the authorities as missing, usually sees her several times a week.
8. After further questioning, Mrs. Harris admitted to me that she had been quite friendly with Mrs. Wallace until they recently argued about trash left in their adjoining hall corridor.
9. However, she firmly stated that her allegations against Mr. Wallace were valid and that she feared repercussions for her actions.

10. At the completion of the interview, I assured Mrs. Harris of the confidentiality of her statements and that an attempt would be made to verify her allegations.
11. However, upon presentation of official identification, Mrs. Wallace refused to admit me to her apartment or grant an interview.
12. As I was leaving Mrs. Harris' apartment, I noticed a man, aged approximately 45, walking out of Mrs. Wallace's apartment.
13. I followed him until he entered a late model green Oldsmobile Cutlass, license plate #238DAB, and sped away.
14. On January 15, I returned to 684 Sunset Street, having determined that Mrs. Wallace is receiving assistance as indicated by Mrs. Harris.
15. I am, therefore, referring this matter to you for further instructions.

John Jones
Senior Investigator

23. The one of the following that indicates the MOST logical order for statements 11 through 15 is

 A. 11, 12, 13, 14, 15
 B. 13, 14, 11, 12, 15
 C. 11, 13, 14, 12, 15
 D. 12, 13, 14, 11, 15

24. Which of the following sentences from the report is ambiguous?
Sentence

 A. 2   B. 7   C. 8   D. 9

25. Of the following, based on the above report and your knowledge of investigative practice, it is MOST likely that investigator Jones failed to obtain the desired information from Mrs. Wallace because

 A. she was aware of Mrs. Harris' allegations
 B. she was fearful of personal injury
 C. he was not operating under cover
 D. he had not made a prior arrangement for the visit

KEY (CORRECT ANSWERS)

1. A
2. A
3. B
4. D
5. A

6. B
7. A
8. B
9. C
10. C

11. B
12. C
13. B
14. B
15. C

16. B
17. B
18. C
19. A
20. D

21. B
22. B
23. D
24. B
25. C

EXAMINATION SECTION
TEST 1

DIRECTIONS: Each question or incomplete statement is followed by several suggested answers or completions. Select the one that BEST answers the question or completes the statement. *PRINT THE LETTER OF THE CORRECT ANSWER IN THE SPACE AT THE RIGHT.*

1. In handling a case, an investigator should summarize the facts he has gathered and the observations he has made about the family and incorporate this material into a formal social study of the family.
Of the following, the CHIEF advantage of such a practice is that it will provide a(n)

    A. picture of the family on the basis of which evaluations and plans can be made
    B. easily accessible listing of the factors pertaining to eligibility
    C. simple and uniform method of recording the family's social history
    D. opportunity for the investigator to record his evaluation of the family's situation

    1.____

2. An applicant for assistance tells the investigator that he has always supported himself by doing odd jobs.
While attempting to verify the applicant's history of past maintenance, it is MOST important for the investigator to determine, in addition,

    A. how the applicant was able to obtain a sufficient number of odd jobs to support himself
    B. what skills the applicant had that enabled him to obtain these jobs
    C. why the applicant never sought or kept a steady job
    D. whether such jobs are still available as a source of income for the applicant

    2.____

3. For an investigator to make a collateral contact with a client's legally responsible relative when that relative is herself receiving assistance is

    A. *advisable*, mainly because the relative may be able to assist the client with needed services
    B. *inadvisable*, mainly because the relative is in receipt of assistance and cannot assist the client financially
    C. *advisable*, mainly because the worker may obtain information concerning the relative's eligibility for assistance
    D. *inadvisable*, because any information concerning the relative can be obtained from other sources

    3.____

4. An applicant for assistance tells the investigator that her bank savings are exhausted. While a bank clearance can verify her statement, it is still important for the investigator to see her bank book CHIEFLY in order to

    A. determine when the account was first opened and the amount of the initial deposit
    B. correlate withdrawals and deposits with the applicant's story of past management
    C. learn if the applicant had closed this account in order to open an account in another bank
    D. verify that the last withdrawal was made before the applicant applied for assistance

    4.____

5. It has been suggested that all investigators be kept currently informed about general departmental actions taken, changes in other departmental work units, and new developments of general interest in their department.
   For a department to put this suggestion into effect is, generally,

   A. *inadvisable;* investigators should perform the duties specifically assigned to them and not get involved in matters that do not concern them directly
   B. *advisable;* investigators may often need to know such information in order to coordinate their work properly with that of other work units
   C. *inadvisable;* changes in other work units have little effect on the work performed by investigators not assigned to these units
   D. *advisable;* broad knowledge of the activities in any agency tends to improve work skills

6. Although there is a normal distinction between the successive ranks of supervision in an agency, the greatest distinction and change in rank occurs, however, when an investigator becomes a supervisor.
   This is true CHIEFLY because the supervisor

   A. must be better informed than his investigators in all aspects
   B. must learn to assume new and more complex duties
   C. becomes responsible for the first time for the job performance of members of the investigation staff
   D. has greater responsibility and authority than the investigators under his supervision

7. When an experienced supervisory investigator does not agree personally with some of the procedurally correct objectives and directions of his supervisor, it would be MOST correct for him to

   A. continue to supervise his unit in accordance with the supervisor's directions
   B. direct his workers to follow the supervisor's directions, but indicate the weaknesses therein and be somewhat more lenient in the supervision of these duties
   C. seek to change the supervisor's directions through use of grievance procedures
   D. develop his own methods and apply them to the work of his unit on a trial basis

8. It has been said that the success or failure of the work of his unit rests on the supervisor.
   If the supervisor wants to stimulate growth among his investigators, it would generally be BEST for him to

   A. set an easy pace for his investigators so that they will not become confused because of having to learn too much too rapidly
   B. set the pace for his investigators so that the job is never too easy but is a constant challenge calling for more and better work
   C. spot check the investigators' records at irregular intervals in order to determine whether they are performing their duties properly
   D. see to it that the broad objectives and goals of the department are periodically communicated and interpreted to his investigators

9. The effectiveness of the work of a unit of investigators depends in a large measure on that unit's will to work.
   The BEST of the following methods for the supervisor to employ in order to increase the will of the members of the unit to work is for the unit supervisor to

A. allow each investigator to proceed at his own pace
B. be constantly on guard for any laxity among his investigators
C. provide comfortable working facilities for his investigators
D. clearly discuss with his investigators the functions and objectives of the agency

10. For a supervisor to encourage his investigators to think about the reasons for a policy is   10._____

    A. *advisable,* mainly because the investigators are then more likely to apply the policy appropriately
    B. *inadvisable,* mainly because the investigators may then apply the policy too flexibly
    C. *advisable,* mainly because the investigators then feel that they have participated in policy making
    D. *inadvisable,* mainly because the investigators may interpret the policy incorrectly if they misunderstand its meaning

11. A supervisor who plans his work properly and who has no difficulty in meeting deadlines insists that his new investigators pattern their activities after his in every detail.   11._____
    This method is

    A. *undesirable,* chiefly because such compliance can cause antagonism and hamper the investigators' growth
    B. *undesirable,* chiefly because this method cannot work as successfully for the new investigators
    C. *desirable,* chiefly because the supervisor's methods have proved successful and will eliminate waste
    D. *desirable,* chiefly because the untrained investigator needs guidelines to follow

12. Of the following, the MOST important reason for obtaining information in an initial investigation regarding financial maintenance of the applicant prior to the application for assistance is to   12._____

    A. comply with the provisions in the Social Welfare Law requiring that a record be made of the financial history of applicants for public assistance
    B. determine if the applicant may be expected to handle properly public assistance grants in the form of money
    C. determine the way in which the present situation differs from the past
    D. show the applicant that the department is interested in his past and present circumstances and may be expected to maintain this interest in the future

13. An applicant for assistance who has legally responsible relatives is informed by the investigator of the responsibility of such relatives to contribute to the applicant's support. The applicant requests permission to discuss the matter privately with these relatives prior to any contact by the department.   13._____
    In this case, it would be ADVISABLE for the investigator to

    A. *agree* to the request because the applicant is entitled to an opportunity to prepare the relatives for the coming official contact
    B. *agree* to the request because the applicant is in a better position than the investigator to uncover any concealment of assets by his relatives
    C. *refuse* the request because it might give the applicant and his relatives opportunity to devise means of avoiding or minimizing the existing responsibility
    D. *refuse* the request because the applicant is not likely to be able to give a proper interpretation to the relatives of their responsibility

14. The findings of a medical examination of a client who has claimed to be unemployable because of physical illness are that the client is employable. When told of these findings, the client reiterates that she is too ill to work.
    In this case, the BEST of the following actions for the investigator to take FIRST is to

    A. discuss the situation with the client in an attempt to discover what reasons she may have for not wanting to accept employment
    B. make arrangements for a psychiatric examination of the client
    C. request that a second medical examination of the client be made by another doctor
    D. tell the client that the case will be closed unless she accepts employment

15. An investigator is told by a relative of a recipient that the recipient has won $6000 in a lottery and is soon to receive the prize money.
    Of the following, the BEST action for the investigator to take FIRST is to

    A. close the case since the recipient did not notify the department of his winnings and since he now has enough money on which to live and pay his bills
    B. discuss the situation with the recipient, planning with him the future management of his funds
    C. let the recipient know that the use of relief money for gambling is illegal and that the police department must be notified of the facts in the case
    D. see that legal steps are taken to recover for services rendered to the client by the department.

16. When told at an interview with the investigator that he must agree to give to the department a lien on his real estate property, a client assumes a resistant attitude.
    Of the following, it would usually be BEST for the investigator to

    A. discuss with the client the laws governing the giving of such liens and the purposes to be served by his giving the lien
    B. drop the matter, hoping to meet with less resistance at some future time
    C. tell the client that this is not a matter for discussion, that he must either agree to the lien or the case will be closed
    D. terminate the interview, telling the client that he may return when he is willing to discuss the means of providing the department with the lien

17. An investigator refers to his supervisor an applicant for assistance who has refused to supply certain information which is regularly asked of applicants. The applicant complains that he is being asked to supply private and personal information about himself that has nothing to do with his application for assistance and that the investigator has treated him with discourtesy.
    The BEST of the following courses of action for the supervisor to take is to

    A. apologize for any appearance of discourtesy but insist that the applicant supply him with the information that had been sought
    B. apologize for any appearance of discourtesy, explain the need for the information that has been requested, and ask the applicant to supply it to the investigator
    C. explain that the investigator is doing a difficult job under difficult conditions and instruct the applicant to cooperate with him
    D. explain why the information is needed and state that no assistance will be forthcoming unless it is supplied

18. At an interview, in order to secure as efficiently as possible the information necessary to determine whether an applicant for assistance is eligible, investigators should generally be instructed to

    A. allow the applicant to explain his problem without interrupting him and then ask him to answer a previously prepared list of detailed questions covering necessary information
    B. confine the interview to a set of detailed questions prepared in advance by the investigator except that new questions may be added on the basis of leads provided by the answers to previous questions
    C. permit the applicant to explain his problems, using questions to keep the applicant from wandering from the subject and to bring out necessary information not covered by him in his narrative
    D. supply the applicant with a set of written questions immediately prior to the interview and confine the interview to a discussion of these questions

18.____

19. Assume that a client believes that his case has been unfairly closed, in spite of the fact that the investigator has explained the pertinent rules to him.
    It would be MOST proper, at this point, for the investigator to refer this client to

    A. an assistant to the commissioner at the central office
    B. an official of the state
    C. the supervisor in charge
    D. the supervisor in charge of the unit

19.____

20. An investigator is told by a client who is a resident of a nursing home that he is being neglected and not receiving proper care in the home.
    The investigator should

    A. discuss the situation with the proprietor of the nursing home
    B. investigate the situation on subsequent visits to determine the validity of the complaint
    C. report the matter to the medical social worker upon return to his center
    D. write a memorandum to the central nursing home service reporting the situation

20.____

21. Modern thinking and research on the efficient conduct of business has developed concepts of democratic supervision and human relations.
    Proper application of these concepts in dealing with investigators USUALLY results in

    A. a reduction in the use of formal discipline
    B. an increase in the use of formal discipline
    C. discarding discipline imposed from without to be completely replaced by self-imposed discipline
    D. elimination of formal discipline in favor of informal discipline

21.____

22. At the first interview between a supervisor and a newly appointed investigator, GREATEST care should be taken to

    A. build toward a satisfactory personal relationship even if some other objectives of the interview must be postponed
    B. cover a predetermined list of specific objectives so as to make a further orientation interview unnecessary

22.____

C. create an image of a forceful, determined supervisor whose wishes cannot be imposed by a subordinate without great risk
D. create an impression of efficiency and control of operation free from interpersonal relationships

23. In teaching the job to an investigator recently assigned to a unit, many teaching methods must be used.
In general, however, the BEST way for the supervisor to train such an investigator is by having him

A. do the job under proper supervision
B. listen to lectures
C. observe the work of other investigators
D. study written material

24. A recently appointed investigator has reached the stage in learning his job where he is just beginning to be able to make decisions, although he still makes numerous mistakes and frequently does not know how to handle a situation.
When the supervisor finds that the investigator has handled a certain situation in an acceptable manner, but not in the best manner, it would be BEST for the supervisor to

A. explain to the investigator how he could have handled the situation better
B. indicate approval of the way the situation was handled and explain how it could have been handled better
C. say nothing about the situation
D. show dissatisfaction with the way the situation was handled and explain how it could have been handled better

25. A supervisor has a job to be done of a type usually done by an investigator. The job is an important and recurring one, but not urgent at the moment. He knows that it would take more time to tell the investigator how to do the job than to do it himself, and that it would take still more time to make the investigator understand the situation, decide how to handle it, and then get the job done.
In such a case, it would generally be BEST for the supervisor to

A. assign the job to the investigator without explaining it
B. do the job himself
C. explain the situation and help the investigator to decide how to handle it
D. tell the investigator exactly what to do

KEY (CORRECT ANSWERS)

1. A
2. D
3. A
4. B
5. B

6. C
7. A
8. B
9. D
10. A

11. A
12. C
13. A
14. A
15. B

16. A
17. B
18. C
19. D
20. D

21. A
22. A
23. A
24. B
25. C

TEST 2

DIRECTIONS: Each question or incomplete statement is followed by several suggested answers or completions. Select the one that BEST answers the question or completes the statement. *PRINT THE LETTER OF THE CORRECT ANSWER IN THE SPACE AT THE RIGHT.*

1. In order to improve the work of an experienced investigator who usually does average work, the one of the following actions which it would generally be BEST for the supervisor to take is to

    A. allow the investigator to be self-directed and unsupervised except where there is a large outlay of money involved
    B. apply strict discipline to any signs of laxness or inattention to duty
    C. carefully list and document every error made by the investigator and inform him of them
    D. use praise as a device to motivate the investigator to do better work

    1.____

2. The one of the following guiding principles to which a supervisor should give MOST consideration when it becomes necessary to discipline an investigator is that

    A. rules should be applied in a fixed and inflexible manner
    B. the discipline should be applied for the purpose of improving the morale of all his investigators
    C. the main benefit to be derived from disciplining one offender is to deter other potential offenders
    D. the nature of the discipline should be such as to improve the future work of the offender

    2.____

3. A unit supervisor notices one of his investigators reading a novel at his desk during working hours. This is the first time that this has happened. The investigator is an experienced employee who does above-average work.
   For the unit supervisor to ignore the situation is GENERALLY

    A. *wise*, since it is never desirable to penalize a good employee because of any single incident
    B. *unwise*, since it may be interpreted by the staff as condoning inattention to work
    C. *wise*, since democratic supervision allows employees leeway to apportion their workday as they see fit
    D. *unwise*, since it is necessary to take strong action at the first sign of insubordination

    3.____

4. When investigators in a particular unit are guilty of infractions, it is the practice of the unit supervisor to give necessary warnings or reprimands in a jocular manner. This practice is GENERALLY

    A. *unwise*, because humorous or jocular aspects should be kept from relationships between supervisors and investigators
    B. *unwise*, because it leaves the investigator unsure of the true intent or extent of the discipline
    C. *wise*, because it makes the investigator realize that there is no personal animosity involved
    D. *wise*, because it reduces the severity of the warning or reprimand

    4.____

5. An experienced investigator complains to his unit supervisor that the latter's continual very close supervision of his work is unnecessary and annoying. The unit supervisor is a recently appointed supervisor.
   In this case, it would generally be BEST for the unit supervisor to

   A. ask the investigator to explain his complaint further, telling him that it will receive consideration, and then re-evaluate his supervisory practices, seeking advice from his own supervisor if necessary
   B. assure the investigator that there had been no intention of singling him out but that, as a subordinate, he will have to get used to new supervisory methods employed by new, wide-awake supervisors
   C. explain to the investigator that it is the job of the unit supervisor to supervise him and that he should understand his role and be able to overcome his annoyance
   D. promise the investigator that the annoying supervisory methods will be discontinued but remind him that the unit supervisor must be respected and looked to for assistance, training, and supervision

6. A unit supervisor becomes aware that one of his investigators has a personal problem which is causing the subordinate considerable concern and is beginning to affect his work.
   Of the following, the action which it would generally be BEST for the unit supervisor to take is to

   A. ignore the matter but, if the investigator brings the matter up, politely tell him that it is not proper for a unit supervisor to discuss personal problems of subordinates
   B. make the investigator aware that he may discuss personal problems with his unit supervisor who will offer whatever assistance he can, compatible with the duties of his job
   C. refer the matter to his own supervisor
   D. indicate that he would like to help solve the problem and insist that the investigator provide full details

7. An investigator who has many personal problems frequently introduces one or more of them into the discussion at conferences with his unit supervisor. He talks of them at some length.
   It would generally be BEST for the unit supervisor to

   A. discuss the problems with the investigator and, as a helping person, assist with their solution
   B. explain that he would like to help solve the problems but that the repeated introduction of them in conferences is interfering with the work of the unit
   C. inform the investigator that his personal problems should not be brought to the office and that it would be improper for the unit supervisor to try to help with them
   D. listen silently to the exposition of the problems made by the investigator and then return to the business at hand without commenting on the problem

8. For the investigator to understand the culture of a family is important CHIEFLY because the

   A. client tends to react to the situation largely in ways derived from attitudes learned at home

B. needs of the entire family cannot be satisfied unless the individual needs of each member are satisfied first
C. client can be treated more effectively when considered as a member of a cultural group rather than a separate individual
D. family can be understood much more readily if the dominant individual motivating it is understood first

9. Emphasis in the practice of casework has shifted from merely providing the client with a practical service, to involving the client in using the service or treatment.
   This statement implies MOST NEARLY that, at present,

   A. casework will attempt to help the client only when it is felt that he will profit from the service
   B. casework is no longer deeply involved in assisting the client in a direct and realistic way
   C. the most important change in casework today has been its shift from helping the client in a practical way to planning for him in a theoretical way
   D. the caseworker or investigator attempts to mobilize the client to active participation in decision-making

9.____

10. In all casework practice, whether it be in an agency or in an institution, the properly prepared case history record is of great importance in the treatment of the client and his problem CHIEFLY because it

    A. gives the supervisory and administrative casework staff reviewing the case a keener understanding of the general sociological and psychological causes underlying dependency and other factors which make it necessary for clients to seek casework assistance
    B. furnishes the agency or institution involved in the case with a factual record as a basis for determining whether or not continuing treatment of the client is justified
    C. assists the caseworkers or investigators involved in the case by providing them, on a continuous basis, with a clear picture of the various factors underlying the client's problems and of what has been done to help resolve the situation
    D. provides the caseworker or investigator responsible for the case with the basic facts which will enable her to determine whether the client is really trying to help himself or whether he is passing his responsibility on to the caseworker or investigator

10.____

11. When comparing the narrative form with the summary form of a casework recording, the narrative form is usually the BEST way to record

    A. objective material obtained from investigations of the client's statements, while the summary form is best to record worker's detailed observations of client's reactions to his present problem
    B. both social data and eligibility material, while the summary form is best to record material dealing with feelings, attitudes and client-worker relationships
    C. material relating to prognosis, treatment given, and the results obtained, while the summary form is best to record a verbatim report of primary evidence obtained from personal worker-client contacts
    D. material dealing with feelings, attitudes, and client-worker relationships, while the summary form is best to record both social data and eligibility material

11.____

12. A problem in recording is to decide how much detail to have in a case record. The case history should GENERALLY include

    A. a more detailed description of the client's reaction to practical matters than to psychological conflicts
    B. a verbatim account of worker-client interaction in significant interviews and a detailed description of the client's feelings toward the treatment plan
    C. only as much data, whether it be sociological or psychological, as will enable the worker to understand the client, the problem to be solved, and the main factors in its solution
    D. the full details of the client's personality development and emotional relationships regardless of the type or complexity of the problem

13. Interviewing is always directed to the client and his situation.
    The one of the following which is the MOST accurate statement with respect to the proper focus of an interview is that the

    A. investigator limits the client to concentration on objective data
    B. client is generally permitted to talk about facts and feelings with no direction from the investigator
    C. main focus in interviews is on feelings rather than facts
    D. investigator is responsible for helping the client focus on any material which seems to be related to his problems or difficulties

14. Assume that you are conducting a training program for the investigators under your supervision. At one of the sessions, you discuss the problem of interviewing a dull and stupid client who gives a slow and disconnected case history.
    The BEST of the following interviewing methods for you to recommend in such a case in order to ascertain the facts is for the investigator to

    A. ask the client leading questions requiring *yes* or *no* answers
    B. request the client to limit his narration to the essential facts so that the interview can be kept as brief as possible
    C. review the story with the client, patiently asking simple questions
    D. tell the client that unless he is more cooperative, he cannot be helped to solve his problem

15. A recent development in interviewing procedure, known as multiple-client interviewing, consists of interviews of the entire family at the same time. However, this may not be an effective method in certain situations.
    Of the following, the situation in which the standard individual interview would be PREFERABLE is when

    A. family members derive consistent and major gratification from assisting each other in their destructive responses
    B. there is a crucial family conflict to which the members are reacting
    C. the family is overwhelmed by interpersonal anxieties which have not been explored
    D. the investigator wants to determine the pattern of family interaction to further his diagnostic understanding

16. The one of the following which is the CHIEF value of verbatim recording of all or a portion of an important interview is the possibility it offers for

    A. careful study and clarification of psychological goals in treatment
    B. a prompt solution to the problem by preservation, in an orderly and concise fashion of the full psychological and economic picture of the client's situation
    C. quick determination of the more obvious social goals and offering of concrete services by presentation of the essential facts
    D. supervision of experienced investigators by showing the emotional overtones, subtle reactions, and intricate investigator-client interchanges

17. Experts in the field of casework recording generally agree that the kind of material for which the narrative form of recording is MOST suitable is

    A. material that deals with feelings, attitudes, and client-investigator relationships, because this style permits the use of primary evidence in the form of verbal material and behavior observed in the interview
    B. social data, including eligibility material and family background history, because it can then be presented in a chronological, orderly fashion to enable the investigator to select the desired facts
    C. personal facts concerning the individual's personality patterns and their growth and development, because they can be seen in an orderly progression from primal immaturity until their ultimate stage of completion
    D. selectively chosen and documented material essential to a quicker and clearer understanding of the various ramifications of the case by a new investigator when responsibility for handling the client is reassigned

18. A case record includes relevant social and psychological facts about the client, the nature of his request, his feeling about his situation, his attitude towards the agency and his use of and reaction to treatment.
    In addition, it should always contain

    A. routine history
    B. complete details of personality development and emotional relationships
    C. detailed process accounts of all contacts
    D. data necessary for understanding the problem and the factors important in arriving at a solution

19. The CHIEF basis for the inability of a troubled client to express his problem clearly to the investigator is that the client

    A. sees his problem in complex terms and does not think it possible to give the investigator the whole picture
    B. has erected defenses against emotions that seem to him inadmissible or intolerable
    C. cannot describe how he feels about his problem
    D. views the situation as unlikely to be solved and is blocked in self-expression

20. In aggressive casework, when an investigator visits a multi-problem family, he should begin by

    A. arranging individual interviews with the children
    B. outlining the steps to be taken in the solution of their problems

C. inviting the family to visit the agency so that a normal casework situation may be created
D. explaining what points of risk or danger exist in their situation and inviting an expression of their feelings

21. The job of the supervisory investigator may be considered in part an administrative one CHIEFLY because it   21.____

    A. requires administrative training or experience
    B. involves a direct relationship with the executive office of the department
    C. entails responsibility for staff development
    D. calls for planning, organizing, and coordinating

22. If a supervisory investigator discovers that the amount of the grant in a particular case is inaccurate, he should   22.____

    A. make the necessary adjustments and assign another investigator to the case
    B. caution all investigators in the unit to be more careful in the future
    C. assume that the investigator's computation was correct when it was made
    D. arrange to have the investigator review the budget with the client and make the necessary adjustments

23. If, in the process of investigating eligibility for assistance, discrepancies occur between the applicant's statement of his situation and that given by a relative interviewed, the investigator should USUALLY   23.____

    A. accept the relative's statement since the relative has less interest in falsifying the facts
    B. return to the client for clarification of the situation
    C. immediately discount the relative's statement since he may be motivated by his legal responsibility for supporting the applicant
    D. point out the discrepancies to the relative and ask him for any explanation he can give

24. In evaluating the adequacy of an individual's income, an investigator should place PRIMARY emphasis on   24.____

    A. its value in relation to the average income
    B. the source of the income
    C. its relation to the earning capacity of the individual
    D. its purchasing power

25. The length of residence required to make a person eligible for the various forms of public assistance available in the United States   25.____

    A. is the same in all states but is different among public assistance programs in a given state
    B. is the same in all states and among different public assistance programs in a given state
    C. is the same in all states for different categories
    D. varies among states and among different public assistance programs in a given state

KEY (CORRECT ANSWERS)

1.	D	11.	D
2.	D	12.	C
3.	B	13.	D
4.	B	14.	C
5.	A	15.	A
6.	B	16.	A
7.	B	17.	A
8.	A	18.	D
9.	D	19.	B
10.	C	20.	D

21. D
22. D
23. B
24. D
25. D

TEST 3

DIRECTIONS: Each question or incomplete statement is followed by several suggested answers or completions. Select the one that BEST answers the question or completes the statement. *PRINT THE LETTER OF THE CORRECT ANSWER IN THE SPACE AT THE RIGHT.*

1. A person who knowingly brings a needy person from another state into the state for the purpose of making him a public charge is guilty of

    A. violation of the Displaced Persons Act
    B. violation of the Mann Act
    C. a felony
    D. a misdemeanor

2. An aged person who is unable to produce immediate proof of age has made an application for assistance. He states that it will take about a week to obtain the necessary proof and that he does not have enough money to provide meals for himself until then.
If it appears that he is in immediate need, he should be told that

    A. temporary assistance will be provided pending the completion of the investigation
    B. a personal loan will be made to him from a revolving fund
    C. he should arrange for a small loan from private sources
    D. he will have to produce an affidavit witnessed by two relatives who will vouch for the accuracy of his statements before any assistance can be provided

3. If the investigator learns during an interview that the client has applied for assistance without the knowledge of her husband, even though he is a member of the same household, the investigator should

    A. appear not to notice this oversight but watch for other evidences of marital discord
    B. make no mention of this to the applicant but, before taking final action, send a note to the husband asking him to come in
    C. discuss this situation with the client and help her recognize the value of her husband's participation in the application
    D. point out to the applicant the implications of her behavior and ask for an explanation of her motives

4. Of the sources through which an agency can seek information about the family background and economic needs of a particular client, the MOST important consists of

    A. records and documents covering the client
    B. interviews with the client's relatives
    C. the client's own story
    D. direct contacts with former employers

5. The one of the following sources of evidence which would be MOST likely to give information needed to verify residence is

    A. family affidavits
    B. medical and hospital bills
    C. an original birth certificate
    D. rental receipts

6. Vital statistics are a resource used by investigators to

    A. help establish eligibility through verification of births, deaths, and marriages
    B. help establish eligibility through verification of divorce proceedings
    C. secure proof of unemployment and eligibility for unemployment compensation
    D. secure indices of the cost of living in the larger cities

7. Case records should be considered confidential in order to

    A. permit investigators to make objective, rather than subjective, comments
    B. prevent recipients from comparing amounts of assistance given to other recipients
    C. keep pertinent information from other investigators
    D. protect clients and their families

8. Because the investigator generally is not trained as a psychiatrist, he should, when encountering psychiatric problems in the performance of his departmental duties,

    A. ignore such problems because they are beyond the scope of his responsibilities
    B. inform the affected persons that he recognizes their problems personally but will take no official cognizance of them
    C. ask to be relieved of the cases in which these problems are met and recommend that they be assigned to a psychiatrist
    D. recognize such problems where they exist and make referrals to the proper sources for treatment

9. Inasmuch as periodic visits to clients at home are required by the department, according to good work practice, it is MOST desirable for the investigator to

    A. visit without appointment as this gives him a chance to see the person and the house *as they really are* and forestalls changing things to create a different impression
    B. write giving an appointment time as this saves the investigator from visiting when people are not at home and helps him to plan his work more efficiently
    C. write suggesting an appointment time so that the client may be prepared for the interview and the investigator uses his time economically
    D. advise all applicants during their first interview that they will be visited periodically but will not be given definite appointments

10. Assuming that careful interpretation has been given but an applicant for assistance refuses to accede to the necessary procedures to establish his eligibility, the MOST preferable of the following courses of action for the investigator to take would be to

    A. do nothing further
    B. grant a temporary delay in the hope that the applicant will change his mind
    C. try to ascertain why the applicant feels as he does, but to respect his decision if he refuses to change his mind
    D. proceed to check on all the facts possible even though the applicant has not given his permission

11. The PRIMARY purpose in discussing with an applicant the steps in determining his eligibility and the kind of verification of facts which the agency will need is to

   A. enable the applicant to understand the basis of eligibility and participate in determining it
   B. protect the position of the agency so that there will be no comeback if the application is not granted
   C. give the applicant an opportunity to modify any statement he may have made previously
   D. promote public relations for the agency since the applicant will tell others how the agency is operating

12. Of the following, the LEAST valid reason for the maintenance of the case record is to

   A. furnish reference material for other investigators
   B. improve the quality of service to the client
   C. show how the funds are being expended
   D. reduce the complexities of the case to manageable proportions

13. A public agency will lean more on forms than a private agency in the same field of activity because

   A. forms simplify the recording responsibilities of newly appointed investigators
   B. public records are of the family agency type
   C. the governmental framework requires a greater degree of standardization
   D. more interviews and visits are made in connection with public cases

14. In spite of the need which most of us have of finding rules and procedures to guide us, we must face the difficulty at the outset that there is no such thing as a model case record.
    Of the following, the BEST justification for this statement is that

   A. records should be written to suit the case
   B. case recording should be patterned after the best models obtainable
   C. rules cannot be applied to case work because each case requires individual treatment
   D. the establishment of routine and procedures in investigatory work is an ideal which cannot be realized

15. In attempting to discover whether an applicant for aid has had any previous experience as a recipient through other agencies in the community, the investigator should

   A. check the application with the social service exchange
   B. send the fingerprints of the applicant to the Police Department
   C. consult the latest records of the department
   D. ask the applicant to submit a notarized statement to the effect that such aid has not been received from any other source

16. Suppose a client whom you are investigating has borrowed $250 in order to purchase an evening gown for one of her children who is being graduated from high school. She is planning to repay the loan at the rate of ten dollars a week and presents verification of this transaction as well as the purchase.
    As an investigator, you would be complying with the BEST casework principles by

A. telling the client her grant will be reduced in view of her ability to manage on ten dollars less each week
B. telling the client that she must never do this again
C. explaining to the client how her action will make it more difficult for the family to get along on their limited grant
D. suggesting that she return the dress and repay the borrowed money in this way

17. An investigator determined, while investigating an applicant for Medical Assistance for the Aged, that the applicant's income and resources are over and above the limits permitted under the Medical Assistance for the Aged program. However, the applicant's medical needs seem to be extensive, and the applicant insists that he cannot pay for his needed medical care.
The investigator should

    A. accept the case for Medical Assistance for the Aged in the normal manner and await a determination of the cost of the medical care in order to determine if there is actually a budget deficit
    B. have the cost of the medical care determined prior to making any decision as to acceptance or rejection of the case
    C. handle the case exactly as he would the case of an applicant for any other type of assistance who does not have a budget deficit
    D. reject the case for Medical Assistance for the Aged until the applicant can obtain verification of the cost of his needed medical care

18. Of the following, the choice of method to be used in the supervisory process should be influenced MOST by the

    A. number and type of cases carried by each investigator
    B. emotional maturity of the investigator
    C. number of investigators supervised and their past experience
    D. subject matter to be learned and the long range goals of supervision

19. In an evaluation conference with an investigator, the BEST approach for the supervisor to take is to

    A. help the investigator to identify his strengths, as a basis for working on his weaknesses
    B. identify the investigator's weaknesses and help him overcome them
    C. allow the investigator to identify his weaknesses first and then suggest ways of overcoming them
    D. discuss the investigator's weaknesses but emphasize his strengths

20. Assume that an investigator is discouraged about the progress of his work and feels that it is futile to attempt to cope with many of his cases.
Of the following, it would be BEST for the supervisor to

    A. suggest to the investigator that such feelings are inappropriate for a professional worker
    B. tell the investigator that he must seek professional help in order to overcome these feelings
    C. reduce the investigator's caseload and give him cases that are less complex
    D. review with the investigator several of his cases in which there were obvious accomplishments

21. The supervisor is responsible for providing the investigator with the following means of support, with the EXCEPTION of

    A. interest and advice on his personal problems
    B. instruction on community resources
    C. inspiration for carrying out the work of the agency
    D. understanding his strengths and limitations

21.____

22. When an investigator frequently takes the initiative in asking questions and discussing problems during a supervisory conference, this is probably an indication that the

    A. supervisor is not sufficiently interested in the investigator
    B. conference is a positive learning experience for the investigator
    C. worker is hostile and resists supervision
    D. supervisor's position of authority is in question

22.____

23. When a supervisor finds that one of his investigators cannot accept criticism, of the following, it would be BEST for the supervisor to

    A. have the investigator transferred to another supervisor
    B. warn the investigator of disciplinary proceedings unless his attitude changes
    C. have the investigator suspended after explaining the reason
    D. explore with the investigator his attitude toward authority

23.____

24. Of the following, the condition which the inexperienced investigator is LEAST likely to be aware of, without the guidance of the supervisor, is

    A. when he is successful in helping a client
    B. when he is not making progress in helping a client
    C. that he has a personal bias toward certain clients
    D. that he feels insecure because of lack of experience

24.____

25. The supervisor should provide an inexperienced investigator with controls as well as freedom MAINLY because controls will

    A. enable him to set up his own controls sooner
    B. put him in a situation which is closer to the realities of life
    C. help him to use authority in handling a casework problem
    D. give him a feeling of security and lay the foundation for future self-direction

25.____

KEY (CORRECT ANSWERS)

1.	D	11.	A
2.	A	12.	D
3.	C	13.	C
4.	C	14.	A
5.	D	15.	A
6.	A	16.	C
7.	D	17.	A
8.	D	18.	D
9.	C	19.	A
10.	C	20.	D

21. A
22. B
23. D
24. C
25. D

EXAMINATION SECTION
TEST 1

DIRECTIONS: Each question or incomplete statement is followed by several suggested answers or completions. Select the one that BEST answers the question or completes the statement. *PRINT THE LETTER OF THE CORRECT ANSWER IN THE SPACE AT THE RIGHT.*

1. The reliability of information obtained increases with the number of persons interviewed. The more the interviewees differ in their statements, the more persons it is necessary to interview to ascertain the true facts.
   According to this statement, the dependability of the information about an occurrence obtained from interviews is related to
   A. how many people are interviewed
   B. how soon after the occurrence an interview can be arranged
   C. the individual technique of the interviewer
   D. the interviewer's ability to detect differences in the statements of interviewees

   1.____

2. A sufficient quantity of the material supplied as evidence enables the laboratory expert to determine the true nature of the substance, whereas an extremely limited specimen may be an abnormal sample containing foreign matter not indicative of the true nature of the material.
   On the basis of this statement alone, it may be concluded that a reason for giving an adequate sample of material for evidence to a laboratory expert is that
   A. a limited specimen spoils more quickly than a larger sample
   B. a small sample may not truly represent the evidence
   C. he cannot analyze a small sample correctly
   D. he must have enough material to keep a part of it untouched to show in court

   2.____

Questions 3-4.

DIRECTIONS: Questions 3 and 4 are to be answered SOLELY on the information given in the following paragraph.

Credibility of a witness is usually governed by his character and is evidenced by his reputation for truthfulness. Personal or financial reasons or a criminal record may cause a witness to give false information to avoid being implicated. Age, sex, physical and mental abnormalities, loyalty, revenge, social and economic status, indulgence in alcohol, and the influence of other persons are some of the many factors which may affect the accuracy, willingness, or ability with which witnesses observe, interpret, and describe occurrences.

3. According to the above paragraph, a witness may, for personal reasons, give wrong information about an occurrence because he

   3.____

A. wants to protect his reputation for truthfulness
B. wants to embarrass the investigator
C. doesn't want to embarrass the investigator
D. doesn't really remember what happened

4. According to the above paragraph, factors which influence the witness of an occurrence may affect
   A. not only what he tells about it but what he was able and wanted to see of it
   B. only what he describes and interprets later but not what he actually sees at the time of the event
   C. what he sees but not what he describes
   D. what he is willing to see but not what he is able to see

5. There are few individuals or organizations on whom some records are not kept. This sentence means MOST NEARLY that
   A. a few organizations keep most of the records on individuals
   B. some of the records on a few individuals are destroyed and not kept
   C. there are few records kept on individuals
   D. there is some kind of record kept on almost every individual

Questions 6-10.

DIRECTIONS: Questions 6 through 10 are to be answered SOLELY on the information given in the following paragraph.

Those statutes of limitations which are of interest to a claim examiner are the ones affecting third party actions brought against an insured covered by a liability policy of insurance. Such statutes of limitations are legislative enactments limiting the time within which such actions at law may be brought. Research shows that such periods differ from state to state and vary within the states with the type of action brought. The laws of the jurisdiction in which the action is brought govern and determine the period within which the action may be instituted, regardless of the place of the cause of action or the residence of the parties at the time of cause of action. The period of time set by a statute of limitations for a tort action starts from the moment the alleged tort is committed. The period usually extends continuously until its expiration, upon which legal action may no longer be brought. However, there is a suspension of the running of the period when a defendant has concealed himself in order to avoid service of legal process. The suspension continues until the defendant discontinues his concealment, and then the period starts running again. A defendant may, by his agreement or conduct, be legally barred from asserting the statute of limitations as a defense to an action. The insurance carrier for the defendant may, by the misrepresentation of the claims man, cause such a bar against use of the statute of limitations by the defendant. If the claim examiner of the insurance carrier has by his conduct or assertion lulled the plaintiff into a false sense of security by false representations, the defendant may be barred from setting up the statute of limitations as a defense.

6. Of the following, the MOST suitable title for the above paragraph is:
   A. Fraudulent Use of the Statute of Limitations
   B. Parties at Interest in a Lawsuit
   C. The Claim Examiner and the Law
   D. The Statute of Limitations in Claims Work

7. The period of time during which a third party action may be brought against an insured covered by a liability policy depends on
   A. the laws of the jurisdiction in which the action is brought
   B. where the cause of action which is the subject of the suit took place
   C. where the claimant lived at the time of the cause of action
   D. where the insured lived at the time of the cause of action

8. Time limits in third party actions which are set by the statutes of limitations described above are
   A. determined by claimant's place of residence at start of action
   B. different in a state for different actions
   C. the same from state to state for the same type of action
   D. the same within a state regardless of type of action

9. According to the above paragraph, grounds which may be legally used to prevent a defendant from using the statute of limitations as a defense in the action described are
   A. defendant's agreement or concealment; a charge of liability for death and injury
   B. defendant's agreement or conduct; misrepresentation by the claims man
   C. fraudulent concealment by claim examiner; a charge of liability for death or injury; defendant's agreement
   D. misrepresentation by claim examiner of carrier; defendant's agreement; plaintiff's concealment

10. Suppose an alleged tort was committed on January 1, 2019 and that the period in which action may be taken is set at three years by the statute of limitations. Suppose further that the defendant, in order to avoid service of legal process, had concealed himself from July 1, 2021 through December 2021.
    In this case, the defendant may not use the statute of limitations as a defense unless action is brought by the plaintiff after
    A. January 1, 2022   B. February 28, 2022
    C. June 30, 2022   D. August 1, 2022

Questions 11-15.

DIRECTIONS: Questions 11 through 15 are to be answered SOLELY on the information given in the following paragraph.

The nature of the interview varies with the aim or the use to which it is put. While these uses vary widely, interviews are basically of three types: fact-finding, informing, and motivating. One of these purposes usually predominates in an interview, but not to the exclusion of the other two. If the main purpose is fact-finding, for example, the interviewer must often motivate the interviewee to cooperate in revealing the facts. A major factor in the interview is the interaction of the personalities of the interviewer and the interviewee. The interviewee may not wish to reveal the facts sought; or even though willing enough to impart them, he may not be able to do so because of a lack of clear understanding as to what is wanted or because of lack of ability to put into words the information he has to give. On the other hand, the interviewer may not be able to grasp and report accurately the facts which the one being interviewed is trying to convey. Also, the interviewer's prejudice may make him not want to get at the real facts or make him unable to recognize the truth.

11. According to the above paragraph, the purpose of an interview
    A. determines the nature of the interview
    B. is usually the same for the three basic types of interviews
    C. is predominantly motivation of the interviewee
    D. is usually to check on the accuracy of facts previously obtained

12. In discussing the use or purpose of an interview, the above paragraph points out that
    A. a good interview should have only one purpose
    B. an interview usually has several uses that are equally important
    C. fact-finding should be the main purpose of an interview
    D. the interview usually has one main purpose

13. According to the above paragraph, an obstacle to the successful interview sometimes attributable to the interviewee is
    A. a lack of understanding of how to conduct an interview
    B. an inability to express himself
    C. prejudice toward the interviewer
    D. too great a desire to please

14. According to the above paragraph, one way in which the interviewer may help the interviewee to reveal the facts sought is to
    A. make him willing to impart the facts by stating clearly the consequences of false information
    B. make sure he understands what information is wanted
    C. motivate him by telling him how important he is in the investigation
    D. tell him what words to use to convey the information wanted

15. According to the above paragraph, bias on the part of the interviewer could
    A. be due to inability to understand the facts being imparted
    B. lead him to report the facts accurately
    C. make the interviewee unwilling to impart the truth
    D. prevent him from determining the facts

Questions 16-20.

DIRECTIONS: Questions 16 through 20 are to be answered SOLELY on the information given in the following paragraph.

PROCEDURE TO OBTAIN REIMBURSEMENT FROM DEPARTMENT OF HEALTH FOR CARE OF PHYSICALLY HANDICAPPED CHILDREN

Application for reimbursement must be received by the Department of Health within 30 days of the date of hospital admission in order that the Department of Hospitals may be reimbursed from the date of admission. Upon determination that patient is physically handicapped, as defined under Chapter 780 of the State Laws, the ward clerk shall prepare seven copies of Department of Health Form A-1 or A-2 Application and Authorization and shall submit six copies to the Institutional Collections Unit. The ward clerk shall also initiate two copies of Department of Health Form B-1 or B-2 Financial and Social Report and shall forward them to the Institutional Collections Unit for completion of Page 1 and routing to the Social Service Division for completion of the Social Summary on Page 2. Social Services Division shall return From B-1 or B-2 to the Institutional Collections Unit which shall forward one copy of Form B-1 or B-2 and six copies of Form A-1 or A-2 to Central Office Division of Collections for transmission to Bureau of Handicapped Children, Department of Health.

16. According to the above paragraph, the Department of Health will pay for hospital care for
    A. children who are physically handicapped
    B. any children who are ward patients
    C. physically handicapped adults and children
    D. thirty days for eligible children

17. According to the procedure described in the above paragraph, the definition of what constitutes a physical handicap is made by the
    A. attending physician
    B. laws of the state
    C. Social Services Division
    D. ward clerk

18. According to the above paragraph, Form B-1 or B-2 is
    A. a three-page form containing detachable pages
    B. an authorization form issued by the Department of Hospitals
    C. completed by the ward clerk after the Social Summary has been entered
    D. sent to the Institutional Collections Unit by the Social Service Division

19. According to the above paragraph, after their return by the Social Service Division, the Institutional Collections Unit keeps
    A. one copy of Form A-1 or A-2
    B. one copy of Form A-1 or A-2 and one copy of Form B-1 or B-2
    C. one copy of Form B-1 or B-2
    D. no copies of Forms A-1 or A-2 or B-1 or B-2

20. According to the above paragraph, forwarding the Application and Authorization to the Department of Health is the responsibility of the
    A. Bureau for Handicapped Children
    B. Central Office Division of Collections
    C. Institutional Collections Unit
    D. Social Service Division

21. An investigator interviews members of the public at his desk. The attitude of the public toward this department will probably be LEAST affected by this investigator's
    A. courtesy   B. efficiency   C. height   D. neatness

22. While you are conducting an interview, the telephone at your desk rings.
    Of the following, it would be BEST for you to
    A. ask the interviewer at the next desk to answer your telephone and take the message for you
    B. excuse yourself, pick up the telephone, and tell the person on the other end you are busy and will call him back later
    C. ignore the ringing telephone and continue with the interview
    D. use another telephone to inform the operator not to put calls through to you while you are conducting an interview

23. An interviewee is at your desk, which is quite near to the desks where other people work. He beckons you a little closer and starts to talk in a low voice as though he does not want anyone else to hear him.
    Under these circumstances, the BEST thing for you to do is to
    A. ask him to speak a little louder so that he can be heard
    B. cut the interview short and not get involved in his problems
    C. explain that people at other desks are not eavesdroppers
    D. listen carefully to what he says and give it consideration

24. In the course of your work, you have developed a good relationship with the clerk in charge of the information section of a certain government agency from which you must frequently obtain information. This agency's procedures require that a number of long complicated forms be prepared by you before the information can be released.
    For you to ask the clerk in charge to release information to you without your presenting the forms would be
    A. *unwise*, mainly because the information so obtained is no longer considered official
    B. *wise*, mainly because a great deal of time will be saved by you and by the clerk
    C. *unwise*, mainly because it may impair the good relations you have established
    D. *wise*, mainly because more information can usually be obtained through friendly contacts

25. Sometimes public employees are offered gifts by members of the public in an effort to show appreciation for acts performed purely as a matter of duty. An investigator to whom such a gift was offered refused to accept it.
    The action of the investigator was
    A. *bad*; the gift should have been accepted to avoid being rude to the person making the offer
    B. *bad*; salaries paid public employees are not high enough to justify such refusals

C. *good*; he should accept such a gift only when he has done a special favor for someone
D. *good*; the acceptance of such gifts may raise doubts as to the honesty of the employee

26. From the point of view of current correct English usage and grammar, the MOST acceptable of the following sentences is:
    A. Each claimant was allowed the full amount of their medical expenses.
    B. Either of the three witnesses is available.
    C. Every one of the witnesses was asked to tell his story.
    D. Neither of the witnesses are right.

27. From the point of view of current correct English usage and grammar, the MOST acceptable of the following sentences is:
    A. Beside the statement to the police, the witness spoke to no one.
    B. He made no statement other than to the police and I.
    C. He made no statement to any one else, aside from the police.
    D. The witness spoke to no one but me.

28. From the point of view of current correct English usage and grammar, the MOST acceptable of the following sentences is:
    A. The claimant has no one to blame but himself.
    B. The boss sent us, he and I, to deliver the packages.
    C. The lights come from mine and not his car.
    D. There was room on the stairs for him and myself.

29. Of the following excerpts, selected from letters, the one which is considered by modern letter writing experts to be the BEST is:
    A. Attached please find the application form to be filled out by you. Return the form to this office at the above address.
    B. Forward to this office your check accompanied by the application form enclosed with this letter.
    C. If you wish to apply, please complete and return the enclosed form with your check.
    D. In reply to your letter of December--, enclosed herewith please find the application form you requested.

30. Which of the following sentences would be MOST acceptable, from the point of view of current correct English usage and grammar, in a letter answering a request for information about eligibility for clinic care?
    A. Admission to this clinic is limited to patients' inability to pay for medical care.
    B. Patients who can pay little or nothing for medical care are treated in this clinic.
    C. The patient's ability to pay for medical care is the determining factor in his admissibility to this clinic.
    D. This clinic is for the patient's that cannot afford to pay or that can pay a little for medical care.

31. A city employee who writes a letter requesting information from a businessman should realize that, of the following, it is MOST important to
    A. end the letter with a polite closing
    B. make the letter short enough to fit on one page
    C. use a form, such as a questionnaire, to save the businessman's time
    D. use a courteous tone that will get the desired cooperation

31.____

Questions 32-35.

DIRECTIONS: Each of Questions 32 through 35 consists of a sentence which may be classified appropriately under one of the following four categories:
A. incorrect because of faulty grammar or sentence structure
B. incorrect because of faulty punctuation
C. incorrect because of faulty capitalization
D. correct

Examine each sentence carefully. Then, in the corresponding space at the right, print the letter preceding the category which is the BEST of the four suggested above. Each incorrect sentence contains only one type of error. Consider a sentence correct if it contains none of the types of errors mentioned, although there may be other correct ways of expressing the same thought.

32. Despite the efforts of the Supervising mechanic, the elevator could not be started.   32.____

33. The U.S. Weather Bureau, weather record for the accident date was checked.   33.____

34. John Jones accidentally pushed the wrong button and then all the lights went out.   34.____

35. The investigator ought to of had the witness sign the statement.   35.____

Questions 36-55.

DIRECTIONS: Each of Questions 36 through 55 consists of a word in capital letters followed by four suggested meanings of the word. For each question, choose the word or phrase which means MOST NEARLY the same as the word in capital letters.

36. ABUT   36.____
    A. abandon   B. assist   C. border on   D. renounce

37. ABSCOND   37.____
    A. draw in   B. give up
    C. refrain from   D. deal off

38. BEQUEATH   38.____
    A. deaden   B. hand down   C. make sad   D. scold

9 (#1)

39. BOGUS
    A. sad   B. false   C. shocking   D. stolen
    39.____

40. CALAMITY
    A. disaster   B. female   C. insanity   D. patriot
    40.____

41. COMPULSORY
    A. binding   B. ordinary   C. protected   D. ruling
    41.____

42. CONSIGN
    A. agree with   B. benefit   C. commit   D. drive down
    42.____

43. DEBILITY
    A. failure   B. legality   C. quality   D. weakness
    43.____

44. DEFRAUD
    A. cheat   B. deny   C. reveal   D. tie
    44.____

45. DEPOSITION
    A. absence   B. publication   C. removal   D. testimony
    45.____

46. DOMICILE
    A. anger   B. dwelling   C. tame   D. willing
    46.____

47. HEARSAY
    A. selfish   B. serious   C. rumor   D. unlikely
    47.____

48. HOMOGENEOUS
    A. human   B. racial   C. similar   D. unwise
    48.____

49. ILLICIT
    A. understood   B. uneven   C. unkind   D. unlawful
    49.____

50. LEDGER
    A. book of accounts   B. editor
    C. periodical   D. shelf
    50.____

51. NARRATIVE
    A. gossip   B. natural   C. negative   D. story
    51.____

52. PLAUSIBLE
    A. reasonable   B. respectful
    C. responsible   D. rightful
    52.____

53. RECIPIENT
    A. absentee   B. receiver   C. speaker   D. substitute
    53.____

54. SUBSTANTIATE
    A. appear for   B. arrange   C. confirm   D. combine
    54.____

55. SURMISE
    A. aim B. break C. guess D. order

Questions 56-60.

DIRECTIONS: In Questions 56 through 60, one of the four words is misspelled. For each question, choose the word which is misspelled.

56. A. absence B. accummulate
    C. acknowledgment D. audible

57. A. benificiary B. disbursement
    C. exorbitant D. incidentally

58. A. inoculate B. liaison C. acquire D. noticable

59. A. peddler B. permissible
    C. persuade D. pertenant

60. A. reconcilation B. responsable
    C. sizable D. substantial

61. Suppose a badly cracked sidewalk, 160 feet long and 14 feet wide, is to be torn up and replaced in four equal sections.
    Each section will have _____ square feet.
    A. 40 B. 220 C. 560 C. 680

62. A businessman pays R dollars a month in rent, has a weekly payroll of P dollars, and a utility bill of U dollars for each two months.
    His annual expenses can be expressed by
    A. 12(R+P+U) B. 52(R+P+U)
    C. 12(R+52P+6U) D. 12(R+4P+2U)

63. An interviewer can interview P number of people in H number of hours, including the time needed to prepare a report on each interview.
    The number of people he can interview in a work week of W hours is represented by
    A. HW/P B. PW/H C. PH/W D. 35H/P

64. Claims investigated by a certain unit total $8,430,000 for the year.
    If the cost of investigating these claims is 17.3 cents per $100, the yearly cost of investigating these claims is MOST NEARLY
    A. $1,450 B. $14,500 C. $145,000 D. $1,450,000

65. Suppose that a business you are investigating presents the following figures:

Year	Net Income	Tax Rate on Net Income
2015	$5,500	2%
2016	$5,500	3%
2017	$6,500	2%
2018	$5,200	2½%
2019	$6,200	3%
2020	$6,800	2½%

According to these figures, it is MOST accurate to say that
A. less tax was due in 2019 than in 2020
B. more tax was due in 2015 than in 2018
C. the same amount of tax was due in 2015 and 2016
D. the same amount of tax was due in 2017 and 2018

66. In 2020, the number of investigations completed in a certain unit had increased 230 over the number completed in 2019, an increase of 10%. In 2021, the number completed decreased 10% from the number completed in 2020. Therefore, the number of investigations completed in 2021 was _____ the number completed in 2019.
A. 23 less than
B. 123 less than
C. 230 more than
D. the same as

67. Assume that during a certain period, Unit A investigated 400 cases and Unit B investigated 300 cases.
If each unit doubled its number of investigations, the proportion of Unit A's investigations to Unit B's investigations would then be _____ it was.
A. twice what
B. one-half as large as
C. one-third larger than
D. the same as

68. In a certain family, the teenage daughter's annual earnings are 5/8 the earnings of her brother and 1/5 the earnings of her father.
If her brother earns $19,200 a year, then her father's annual earnings are
A. $60,000   B. $75,000   C. $80,000   D. $96,000

69. Assume that, of the 1,700 verifications made by a certain investigating unit in a one-week period, 40% were birth records, 30% were military records, 10% were citizenship records, and the remainder were miscellaneous records. Then, the MOST accurate of the following statements about the relative number of different records is that
A. citizenship records verifications equaled 20% of military record verifications
B. fewer than 700 verifications were birth records
C miscellaneous records verifications were 20% more than citizenship records verifications
D. more than 550 verifications were military records

70. Two units, A and B, answer, respectfully, 1,000 and 1,500 inquiries a month. Assuming that the number of inquiries answered by Unit A increase at the rate of 20 each month, while those answered by Unit B decrease at the rate of 5 each month, the two units will answer the same number of inquiries at the end of _____ months.
    A. 10   B. 15   C. 20   D. 25

71. The interview is only one of the many investigational techniques used by the investigator for gathering information and evidence. Each such technique has its special use.
    The investigator usually finds the interview MOST suitable for getting
    A. facts or leads which are available only through individuals
    B. information available in documents and public records
    C. physical evidence relating to the subject of investigation
    D. information that people hesitate to put into writing

72. An investigator should consult his supervisor on a complicated problem before going ahead with his investigation.
    For an investigator to follow this advice would be
    A. *bad*, mainly because consultation is an admission of the investigator's weakness
    B. *good*, mainly because consultation is likely to lead to additional ideas on how to solve the problem
    C. *bad*, mainly because supervisors don't have time to discuss every problem with each investigator
    D. *good*, mainly because the responsibility for the investigation is shared with the supervisor

73. The general demeanor of the person being interviewed, what he says, and the way in which he says it, will usually give the investigator reliable clues concerning his character.
    It may be concluded from this statement that
    A. investigators usually become well-versed in applied psychology
    B. the behavior of the interviewee may give some indication of his character
    C. the investigator should be particularly on guard against deceit
    D. reliable people always show such reliability in their demeanor

74. Under the city charter, it is incumbent upon the Commissioner of Hospitals to collect for the care and maintenance of a patient in an institution under the jurisdiction of the Department if such patient is able to pay in whole or in part for such care and maintenance.
    According to the preceding statement, it is MOST reasonable to assume that
    A. city hospitals are largely self-sufficient, medical services being donated and operating expenses being derived from income from patients
    B. city hospital facilities are intended for use only by the medically needy
    C. the duty of the Department of Hospitals to charge patients who are able to pay has a legal basis
    D. the majority of patients in city institutions will not willingly pay for their care and consistent efforts must be made to collect

75. In an experiment, a large group of people witnessed a certain incident. Half of the group was then asked to write a detailed narrative report of what they had seen, while the other half was given a lengthy questionnaire report on the incident to fill out. It was found that the narrative reports covered a greater range of items and contained fewer errors of fact than the question-answer reports.
It is MOST logical to conclude that in this experiment,
   A. narrative report tended to be more accurate than question-answer reports
   B. question-answer reports tended to provide more details, while the narrative reports contained more misstatements of fact
   C. some uncontrolled factor was at work since questionnaires usually elicit much more information than this
   D. the range of questions in the questionnaire was narrow

75.____

76. During the course of an interview, it would be LEAST desirable for the investigator to
   A. correct immediately any grammatical errors made by an interviewee
   B. express himself in such a way as to be clearly understood
   C. restrict the interviewee to the subject of the interview
   D. make notes in a way that will not disturb the interviewee

76.____

77. Municipal hospitals which provide no services for private and semi-private patients shall admit only medically needy persons unless refusal to admit a patient will constitute a hazard to the public health or result in possible danger to the patient's life.
According to this statement, it is MOST logical to assume that
   A. medically needy persons may receive full medical services only in municipal hospitals
   B. no municipal hospitals provide services for private and semi-private patients
   C. services for private and semi-private patients are provided by some municipal hospitals
   D. voluntary and private hospitals provide services only for private and semi-private patients

77.____

78. An investigator is making a neighborhood investigation to find additional witnesses to an automobile accident that happened the day before at a corner in a district of buildings with stores and offices above the stores. He started at 12 noon and stopped at a lunch counter and every store in the vicinity of the accident that was open at the time of the accident.
The investigator's procedure is
   A. *good*; he is likely to find people who were near the scene when the accident happened
   B. *good*; he will find the facts needed in the investigation
   C. *bad*; the investigator should have called first at the offices above the stores, as the view was better from there
   D. *bad*; it is unlikely that people occupied with their business would notice an auto accident outside

78.____

79. An investigator is interviewing a witness who has a speech difficulty. The witness is becoming embarrassed because he has made several errors in telling his story.
Under these circumstances, it would be BEST for the investigator to
   A. call these errors rather sharply to the witness' attention so that he will use greater care in describing the accident
   B. close the interview abruptly in order not to embarrass the witness further
   C. go through the motions of an interview for a while and then close it because this is an unreliable witness
   D. try to ease his embarrassment and help him express himself

80. Some investigators prefer to type a statement to be signed by a witness. Others prefer to write it out in longhand.
One advantage of the handwritten statement as compared with a typewritten statement is that a handwritten statement usually
   A. can be taken immediately while a typed statement cannot
   B. appears to be composed by the witness and so is more reliable
   C. eliminates any future question in court as to who prepared the statement
   D. is not likely to contain as many errors as a statement typed under stress

81. Some testimony cannot be accepted as a fact because the witness could not have perceived personally the events he offers as facts in his testimony.
On this basis, which of the following statements by a witness is MOST acceptable as fact?
   A. "Mr. Brown couldn't hear the horn."
   B. "He intended to call his wife."
   C. "There was no one at his home when he phoned."
   D. "The sidewalk was broken in the spot where he fell."

82. Strategy refers to the general plan or arrangement of the interview; tactics, to what is said or done in the presence of the person being interviewed.
According to this definition, the one of the following which would be an example of interview strategy is
   A. deciding the type of questions to be asked at the interview
   B. maintaining a sincere and reasonable manner
   C. stating the purpose of the interview clearly and simply
   D. wording a question precisely so that there is no misunderstanding as to what is meant

83. The prognosis of the patient's condition is the
   A. description of the patient's present condition
   B. opinion of the major cause of the illness
   C. statement of the expected course of the illness
   D. summary of secondary conditions

84. If a person's employment record indicates that he has never kept a job for any length of time, it is MOST likely that this person is a(n)
   A. part-time worker
   B. trouble maker
   C. unskilled worker
   D. unstable worker

85. In order to help a witness who has had very little education fully understand a statement he is to sign, the investigator, preparing the statement, should
    A. have a notary public witness the preparation and signing of the statement
    B. typewrite the statement since uneducated persons find it hard to read handwritten statements
    C. use legal type questions and answers that are to the point
    D. use the same kind of language that the witness usually speaks

86. Mr. Brown acted out what he had seen happen and described what he was doing by saying, "*Richards was here. The door opened and hit him here—like this.*" The investigator who was recording the interview on tape at his office, said, "*Let me get this straight, Mr. Brown. Richards was standing sideways, two feet from the door, when the door opened, hitting Richard's elbow. Have I got it straight?*" The witness replied, "*Right.*"
    The statement of the investigator under these circumstances was
    A. *bad*; it put words into the mouth of the witness
    B. *bad*; it merely duplicated what the witness had already shown
    C. *good*; it clarified a point that could confuse a listener to the tape
    D. *good*; it showed who was doing the interviewing

87. A significant fact to be remembered by the investigator in the course of his work is that a signed statement by a witness becomes evidence which
    A. can be used later to discredit any major change in the witness's story
    B. cannot be contradicted by other evidence
    C. cannot be used to induce the claimant to agree to a fair settlement
    D. s acceptable in court only if the signer cannot testify in court

88. Which of the following would usually be the BEST question for an investigator to ask a witness to find out what time he got to work?
    A. Did you get to work about 9 o'clock that morning?
    B. I suppose you arrived at the office late that morning?
    C. When did you get to work that day?
    D. You arrived at work late that morning. Can you tell me what time, please?

89. An investigator is examining the application of a 30-year-old applicant for a position.
    Which of the following in his employment history for the past three years would indicate the LEAST need for further investigation of this man's reliability as an employee?
    A. Many changes of employment, each to a position in another state at an equivalent salary
    B. Frequent changes of employment to positions requiring skills the man had never exercised before
    C. Few changes of employment but each change followed by six or more months of unemployment
    D. Few changes of employment, each to a higher salary, with no unemployment

90. Security requirements for employment in defense plants have greatly expanded the number of sources of information about individuals.
   According to the above statement, it is MOST valid to assume that
   A. increased sources of information exist for former defense plant employees
   B. detailed information is available on former defense plant employees
   C. information on former defense plant employees is limited to security information
   D. not much information is available on individuals who never worked in defense plants

90._____

KEY (CORRECT ANSWERS)

1.	A	21.	C	41.	A	61.	C	81.	D
2.	B	22.	B	42.	C	62.	C	82.	A
3.	C	23.	D	43.	D	63.	B	83.	C
4.	A	24.	C	44.	A	64.	B	84.	D
5.	D	25.	D	45.	D	65.	D	85.	D
6.	D	26.	C	46.	B	66.	A	86.	C
7.	A	27.	D	47.	C	67.	D	87.	A
8.	B	28.	A	48.	C	68.	A	88.	C
9.	B	29.	C	49.	D	69.	B	89.	D
10.	C	30.	B	50.	A	70.	C	90.	A
11.	A	31.	D	51.	D	71.	A		
12.	D	32.	C	52.	A	72.	B		
13.	B	33.	B	53.	B	73.	B		
14.	B	34.	D	54.	C	74.	C		
15.	D	35.	A	55.	C	75.	A		
16.	A	36.	C	56.	B	76.	A		
17.	B	37.	D	57.	A	77.	C		
18.	D	38.	B	58.	D	78.	A		
19.	C	39.	B	59.	D	79.	D		
20.	B	40.	A	60.	B	80.	C		

EXAMINATION SECTION
TEST 1

DIRECTIONS: Each question or incomplete statement is followed by several suggested answers or completions. Select the one that BEST answers the question or completes the statement. *PRINT THE LETTER OF THE CORRECT ANSWER IN THE SPACE AT THE RIGHT.*

Questions 1-9.

DIRECTIONS: Questions 1 through 9 measure your ability to (1) determine whether statements from witnesses say essentially the same thing, and (2) determine the evidence need to make it reasonably certain that a particular conclusion is true.

1. Which of the following pairs of statements say essentially the same thing in two different ways?
   I. The only time the machine's red light is on is when the door is locked.
      If the machine's door is locked, the red light is on.
   II. Some gray-jacketed cables are connected to the blower.
      If a cable is connected to the blower, it must be gray-jacketed.
   The CORRECT answer is:
   A. I only   B. I and II   C. II only   D. Neither I nor II   1.____

2. Which of the following pairs of statements say essentially the same thing in two different ways?
   I. If you live on Maple Street, your child is in the Valley District.
      If your child is in the Valley District, you must live on Maple Street.
   II. All the Smith children are brown-eyed.
      If a child is brown-eyed, it is not one of the Smith children.
   The CORRECT answer is:
   A. I only   B. I and II   C. II only   D. Neither I nor II   2.____

3. Which of the following pairs of statements say essentially the same thing in two different ways?
   I. If it's Monday, Mrs. James will be here.
      Mrs. James is here every Monday.
   II. Most people in the Drama Club do not have stage fright, but everyone in the Drama Club wants to be noticed.
      Some people in the Drama Club have stage fright and want to be noticed.
   The CORRECT answer is:
   A. I only   B. I and II   C. II only   D. Neither I nor II   3.____

4. Which of the following pairs of statements say essentially the same thing in two different ways?
   I. If you are older than 65, you will get a senior's discount.
      Either you will get a senior's discount, or you are not older than 65.
   II. Every cadet in Officer Johnson's class has passed the firearms safety course.
       No cadet that has failed the firearms safety course is in Officer Johnson's class.
   The CORRECT answer is:
   A. I only   B. I and II   C. II only   D. Neither I nor II

5. Summary of Evidence Collected to Date:
   Most people in the Greenlawn housing project do not have criminal records.
   Prematurely Drawn Conclusion:
   Some people in Greenlawn who have been crime victims have criminal records themselves.
   Which of the following pieces of evidence, if any, would make it *reasonably certain* that the conclusion drawn is TRUE?
   A. Some of those who live in the Greenlawn project have been arrested or convicted of "victimless" crimes.
   B. Most people in Greenlawn have been the victims of crime.
   C. Everyone in Greenlawn has been the victim of crime.
   D. None of the above

6. Summary of Evidence Collected to Date:
   Every drug dealer in the Oak Lawn neighborhood wears blue and carries a Glock.
   Prematurely Drawn Conclusion:
   A person in the Oak Lawn neighborhood who carries a Glock is a drug dealer.
   Which of the following pieces of evidence, if any, would make it *reasonably certain* that the conclusion drawn is TRUE?
   A. In the Oak Lawn neighborhood, only drug dealers wear blue.
   B. Drug dealers in Oak Lawn only carry Glocks when they're dealing drugs.
   C. In the Oak Lawn neighborhood, only drug dealers carry Glocks.
   D. None of the above

7. Summary of Evidence Collected to Date:
   I. Dr. Jones is older than Dr. Gupta.
   II. Dr. Gupta and Dr. Unruh were born on the same day.
   Prematurely Drawn Conclusion:
   Dr. Gupta does not work in the emergency room.
   Which of the following pieces of evidence, if any, would make it *reasonably certain* that the conclusion drawn is TRUE?
   A. Dr. Jones is older than Dr. Unruh.
   B. Dr. Jones works in the emergency room.
   C. Every doctor in the emergency room is older than Dr. Unruh.
   D. None of the above

3 (#1)

8. Summary of Evidence Collected to Date:
   I. On the street, a "dose" of a certain drug contains four "drams."
   II. A person can trade three "rolls" of a drug for a "plunk."
   Prematurely Drawn Conclusion:
   A plunk is the most valuable amount of the drug on the street.
   Which of the following pieces of evidence, if any, would make it *reasonably certain* that the conclusion drawn is TRUE?
   A. A person can trade five doses for two rolls.
   B. A dram contains two rolls.
   C. A roll is larger than a dram.
   D. None of the above

   8.____

9. Summary of Evidence Collected to Date:
   Sam is a good writer and editor.
   Prematurely Drawn Conclusion:
   Sam is qualified for the job.
   Which of the following pieces of evidence, if any, would make it *reasonably certain* that the conclusion drawn is TRUE?
   A. The job calls for good writing and editing skills.
   B. A person who is not a good editor could still apply for the job on the strength of his/her writing skills.
   C. If Sam applies for the job, he must be both a good writer and editor.
   D. None of the above

   9.____

Questions 10-14.

DIRECTIONS: Questions 10 through 14 refer to Map #7 and measure your ability to orient yourself within a given section of town, neighborhood or particular area. Each of the questions describes a starting point and a destination. Assume that you are driving a car in the area shown on the map accompanying the questions. Use the map as a basis for the shortest way to get from one point to another without breaking the law.
On the map, a street marked by arrows, or by arrows and the words "One Way," indicates one-way travel, and should be assumed to be one-way for the entire length, even when there are breaks or jogs in the street. EXCEPTION: A street that does not have the same name over the full length.

4 (#1)

Map #7.

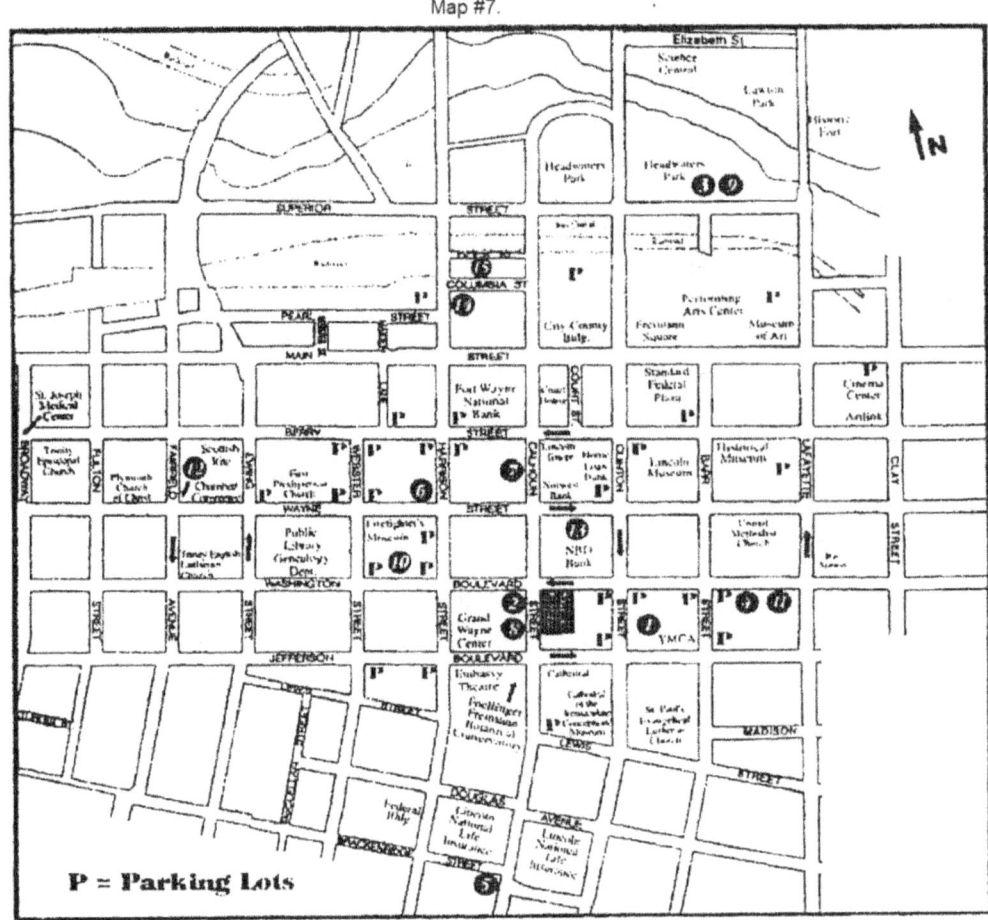

10. The SHORTEST legal way from Trinity Episcopal Church to Science Central is   10.____
    A. east on Berry, north on Clinton, east on Elizabeth
    B. east on Berry, north on Lafayette, west on Elizabeth
    C. north on Fulton, east on Main, north on Lafayette, west on Elizabeth
    D. north on Fulton, east on Main, north on Calhoun

11. The SHORTEST legal way from the Grand Wayne Center to the Museum of   11.____
    Art is
    A. north on Harrison, east on Superior, south on Lafayette
    B. east on Washington Blvd., north on Lafayette
    C. east on Jefferson Blvd., north on Clinton, east on Main
    D. east on Jefferson Blvd., north on Lafayette

12. The SHORTEST legal way from the Embassy Theatre too the City/County   12.____
    Building is
    A. west on Jefferson Blvd., north on Ewing, east on Main
    B. east on Jefferson Blvd., north on Lafayette, west on Main
    C. east on Jefferson Blvd., north on Clinton
    D. north on Harrison, east on Main

54

13. The SHORTEST legal way from the YMCA to the Firefighter's Museum is 13._____
    A. west on Jefferson Blvd., north on Webster
    B. north on Barr, west on Washington Blvd., north on Webster
    C. north on Barr, west on Wayne
    D. north on Barr, west on Berry, south on Webster

14. The SHORTEST legal way from the Historic Fort to Freimann Square is 14._____
    A. north on Lafayette, west on Elizabeth, south on Clinton
    B. north on Lafayette, west on Elizabeth, west/south on Calhoun, east on Main
    C. south on Lafayette, west on Main
    D. south on Lafayette, west on Superior, south on Clinton

Questions 15-19.

DIRECTIONS: Questions 15 through 19 refer to Figure #7, on the following page, and measure your ability to understand written descriptions of events. Each question presents a description of an accident or event and asks you which of the five drawings in Figure #7 BEST represents it.

In the drawings, the following symbols are used:

Moving Vehicle: ◊   Non-moving Vehicle: ■

Pedestrian or Bicyclist: ●

The path and direction of travel of a vehicle or pedestrian is indicated by a solid line.

The path and direction of travel of each vehicle or pedestrian directly involved in a collision from the point of impact is indicated by a dotted line.

In the space at the right, print the letter of the drawing that BEST fits the descriptions written below:

15. A driver headed northeast on Cary strikes a car in the intersection and is 15._____
    diverted north, where he collides with the rear of a car that is traveling north on Park. The northbound car is knocked into the rear of another car that is traveling north ahead of it.

16. A driver headed northeast on Cary strikes a car in the intersection and is 16._____
    diverted north, where he collides head-on with a car stopped at a traffic light in the southbound lane on Park.

17. A driver headed northeast on Cary strikes a car in the intersection and is 17._____
    diverted east, where he collides head-on with a car stopped at a traffic light in the westbound lane on Roble.

18. A driver headed east on Roble collides with the left front of a car that is turning right from Knox onto Roble. The driver swerves right after the collision and collides head-on with another car headed north on Park.   18.____

19. A driver headed northeast on Cary strikes a car in the intersection and is diverted north, where he collides with the rear of a car parked on the northbound lane on Park.   19.____

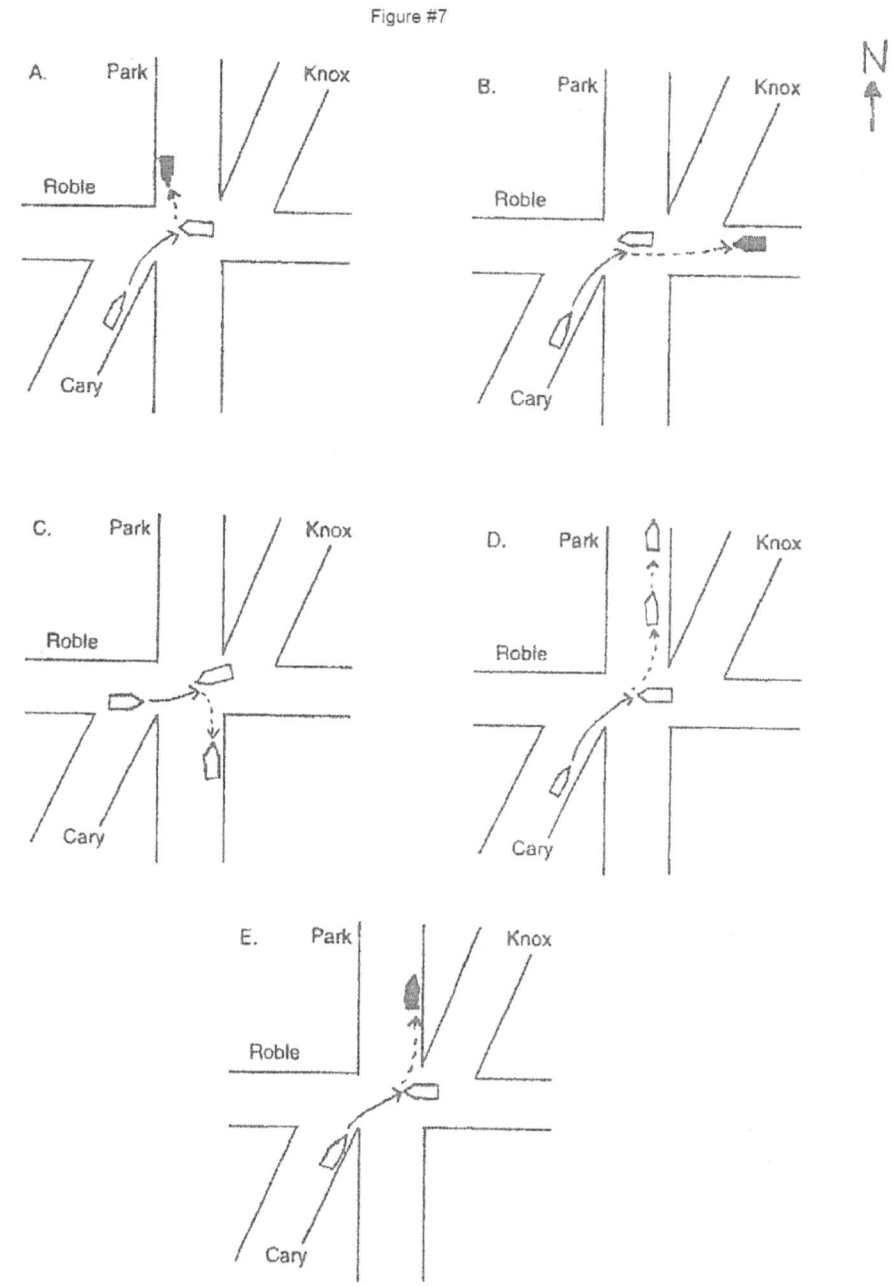

Figure #7

Questions 20-22.

DIRECTIONS: In Questions 20 through 22, choose the word or phrase CLOSEST in meaning to the word or phrase printed in capital letters.

20. JURISDICTION
    A. authority   B. decision   C. judgment   D. argument

21. PROXY
    A. neighbor   B. agent   C. enforcer   D. impostor

22. LARCENY
    A. theft   B. assault   C. deceit   D. gentleness

Questions 23-25.

DIRECTIONS: Questions 22 through 25 measure your ability to do fieldwork-related arithmetic. Each question presents a separate arithmetic problem for you to solve.

23. Mr. Long has 14 employees. He has four more male employees than female employees.
    How many female employees does he have?
    A. 4   B. 5   C. 9   D. 10

24. A box of latex gloves costs $18. A crate has 12 boxes, each of which contains 48 gloves.
    How much does a crate of latex gloves cost?
    A. $216   B. $328   C. $576   D. $864

25. In a single week, the Department of Parking collected 540 quarter, 623 dimes, and 146 nickels from its parking meters.
    What was the TOTAL revenue collected from the meters during the week?
    A. $135.00   B. $154.00   C. $204.60   D. $270.30

KEY (CORRECT ANSWERS)

1. A
2. D
3. B
4. B
5. C

6. C
7. C
8. A
9. A
10. C

11. D
12. D
13. B
14. A
15. D

16. A
17. B
18. C
19. E
20. A

21. B
22. A
23. B
24. A
25. C

SOLUTIONS (QUESTIONS 1-9)

P implies Q = original statement

Not Q implies not P = contrapositive of the original statement. A statement and its contrapositive are logically equivalent.

Q implies P = converse of the original statement.

Not P implies not Q = inverse of the original statement. The converse and inverse of an original statement are logically equivalent.

P implies Q = Not P or Q

1. CORRECT ANSWER: A
   For Item I, the equivalent of the first statement would be "If the red light is on, the door is locked." This is the converse of the second statement, so it is not equivalent to the first statement. For Item II, the first statement does not guarantee that all cables that are connected to the blower must be gray-jacketed. There may very well be other cables that are connected to the blower that are not gray-jacketed. Equally possible, some gray-jacketed cables are not necessarily connected to the blower.

2. CORRECT ANSWER: D
   For Item I, the second statement is the converse of the first statement, so it is not logically equivalent. For Item II, the equivalent of the first statement is "If a child is not brown-eyed, then it is not one of the Smith children." Thus, statement II as it stands is not equivalent to statement I.

3. CORRECT ANSWER: B
   For Item I, Mrs. James is here every Monday, so we conclude that if it is Monday, she is here. (She may be here on other days as well.) For Item II, we can conclude that there are some people in the Drama Club who do have stage fright. Since everyone in the Drama Club wants to be noticed, this would include those who have stage fright.

4. CORRECT ANSWER: B
   For Item I, these two statements represent "P implies Q" and "Not P or Q," where P = Older than 65 and Q = Get a senior discount. These are equivalent statements. For Item II, these statements are contrapositive of each other and so must be equivalent. (P = Cadet in Johnson's class and Q = Passes the safety course.)

5. CORRECT ANSWER: C
   If everyone in the housing project has been a victim of crime and most of these people do not have a criminal record, we can conclude that some of them do have a criminal record. Thus, we have the situation that some of the people who live in this housing project are both a victim of crime as well as a perpetrator of crime.

6. CORRECT ANSWER: C
   This choice can be written as "In this neighborhood, if a person carries a Glock, he is a drug dealer." This would lead directly to the drawn conclusion.

7. CORRECT ANSWER: C
   We know that every doctor in the emergency room is older than Dr. Unruh; it is not possible for Dr. Gupta to be working in the emergency room since he is the same age as Dr. Unruh.

8. CORRECT ANSWER: A
   From statement I, a dose is worth more than a dram. If 5 doses is equal to 2 rolls, then a roll is worth more than a dose. So of these three, a roll is worth the most. Finally, statement II tells us that a plunk is worth more than a roll. This means that a plunk is worth the most among all four of these categories.

9. CORRECT ANSWER: A
   Sam has the qualifications of being a good writer and editor, which is exactly what is needed for the job. Therefore, Sam is qualified for this job.

TEST 2

DIRECTIONS: Each question or incomplete statement is followed by several suggested answers or completions. Select the one that BEST answers the question or completes the statement. *PRINT THE LETTER OF THE CORRECT ANSWER IN THE SPACE AT THE RIGHT.*

Questions 1-9.

DIRECTIONS: Questions 1 through 9 measure your ability to (1) determine whether statements from witnesses say essentially the same thing, and (2) determine the evidence need to make it reasonably certain that a particular conclusion is true.

To do well on this part of the test, you do NOT have to have a working knowledge of police procedures and techniques. Nor do you have to have any more familiarity with criminals and criminal behavior than that acquired from reading newspapers, listening to radio or watching TV. To do well in this part, you must read and reason carefully.

1. Which of the following pairs of statements say essentially the same thing in two different ways?
   I. If the garbage is collected today, it is definitely Wednesday.
      The garbage is collected every Wednesday.
   II. Nobody has no answer to the question.
      Everybody has at least one answer to the question.
   The CORRECT answer is:
   A. I only   B. I and II   C. II only   D. Neither I nor II

   1.____

2. Which of the following pairs of statements say essentially the same thing in two different ways?
   I. If it trains, the streets will be wet.
      If the streets are wet, it has rained.
   II. All of the Duluth Five are immune from prosecution.
      No member of the Duluth Five can be prosecuted.
   The CORRECT answer is:
   A. I only   B. I and II   C. II only   D. Neither I nor II

   2.____

3. Which of the following pairs of statements say essentially the same thing in two different ways?
   I. Ms. Friar will accept her promotion if and only if she is offered a 10% raise.
      For Ms. Friar to accept her promotion, it is necessary that she be offered a 10% raise.
   II. If the hydraulic lines are flushed, it is definitely inspection day.
      The hydraulic lines are flushed only on inspection days.
   The CORRECT answer is:
   A. I only   B. I and II   C. II only   D. Neither I nor II

   3.____

61

4. Which of the following pairs of statements say essentially the same thing in two different ways?
   I. If you are tall you will get onto the basketball team.
      Unless you are tall, you will not get onto the basketball team.
   II. That raven is black.
      If that bird is black, it's a raven.
   The CORRECT answer is:
   A. I only   B. I and II   C. II only   D. Neither I nor II

5. Summary of Evidence Collected to Date:
   Every member of the Rotary Club is retired.
   Prematurely Drawn Conclusion:
   At least some people in the planning commission are retired.
   Which of the following pieces of evidence, if any, would make it *reasonably certain* that the conclusion drawn is TRUE?
   A. Retirement is a condition for membership in the Rotary Club.
   B. Every member of the planning commission has been in the Rotary Club at one time.
   C. Every member of the Rotary Club is also on the planning commission.
   D. None of the above

6. Summary of Evidence Collected to Date:
   Some of the SWAT team snipers have poor aim.
   Prematurely Drawn Conclusion:
   The snipers on the SWAT team with the worst aim also have 20/20 vision.
   Which of the following pieces of evidence, if any, would make it *reasonably certain* that the conclusion drawn is TRUE?
   A. Some of the SWAT team snipers have 20/20 vision.
   B. Every sniper on the SWAT team has 20/20 vision.
   C. Some snipers on the SWAT team wear corrective lenses.
   D. None of the above

7. Summary of Evidence Collected to Date:
   The only time Garson hears voices is on a day when he doesn't take his medication.
   Prematurely Drawn Conclusion:
   On Fridays, Garson never hears voices.
   Which of the following pieces of evidence, if any, would make it *reasonably certain* that the conclusion drawn is TRUE?
   A. Garson is supposed to take his medication every day.
   B. Garson usually undergoes shock therapy on Fridays.
   C. Garson usually takes his medication and undergoes shock therapy on Fridays.
   D. None of the above

8. <u>Summary of Evidence Collected to Date:</u>
   Among the three maintenance workers, Frank, Lily and Jean, Frank is not the tallest.
   <u>Prematurely Drawn Conclusion:</u>
   Lily is the tallest.
   Which of the following pieces of evidence, if any, would make it *reasonably certain* that the conclusion drawn is TRUE?
   - A. Jean is not the tallest.
   - B. Frank is the shortest.
   - C. Jean is the shortest.
   - D. None of the above

9. <u>Summary of Evidence Collected to Date:</u>
   Doctor Lyons went to the cafeteria for lunch today and did not eat dessert.
   <u>Prematurely Drawn Conclusion:</u>
   The cafeteria did not serve dessert.
   Which of the following pieces of evidence, if any, would make it *reasonably certain* that the conclusion drawn is TRUE?
   - A. Dr. Lyons never eats dessert.
   - B. When the cafeteria serves dessert, Dr. Lyons always eats it.
   - C. The cafeteria rarely serves dessert when Dr. Lyons eats there.

Questions 10-14.

DIRECTIONS: Questions 10 through 14 refer to Map #8 and measure your ability to orient yourself within a given section of town, neighborhood or particular area. Each of the questions describes a starting point and a destination. Assume that you are driving a car in the area shown on the map accompanying the questions. Use the map as a basis for the shortest way to get from one point to another without breaking the law.
On the map, a street marked by arrows, or by arrows and the words "One Way," indicates one-way travel, and should be assumed to be one-way for the entire length, even when there are breaks or jogs in the street. EXCEPTION: A street that does not have the same name over the full length.

Map #8

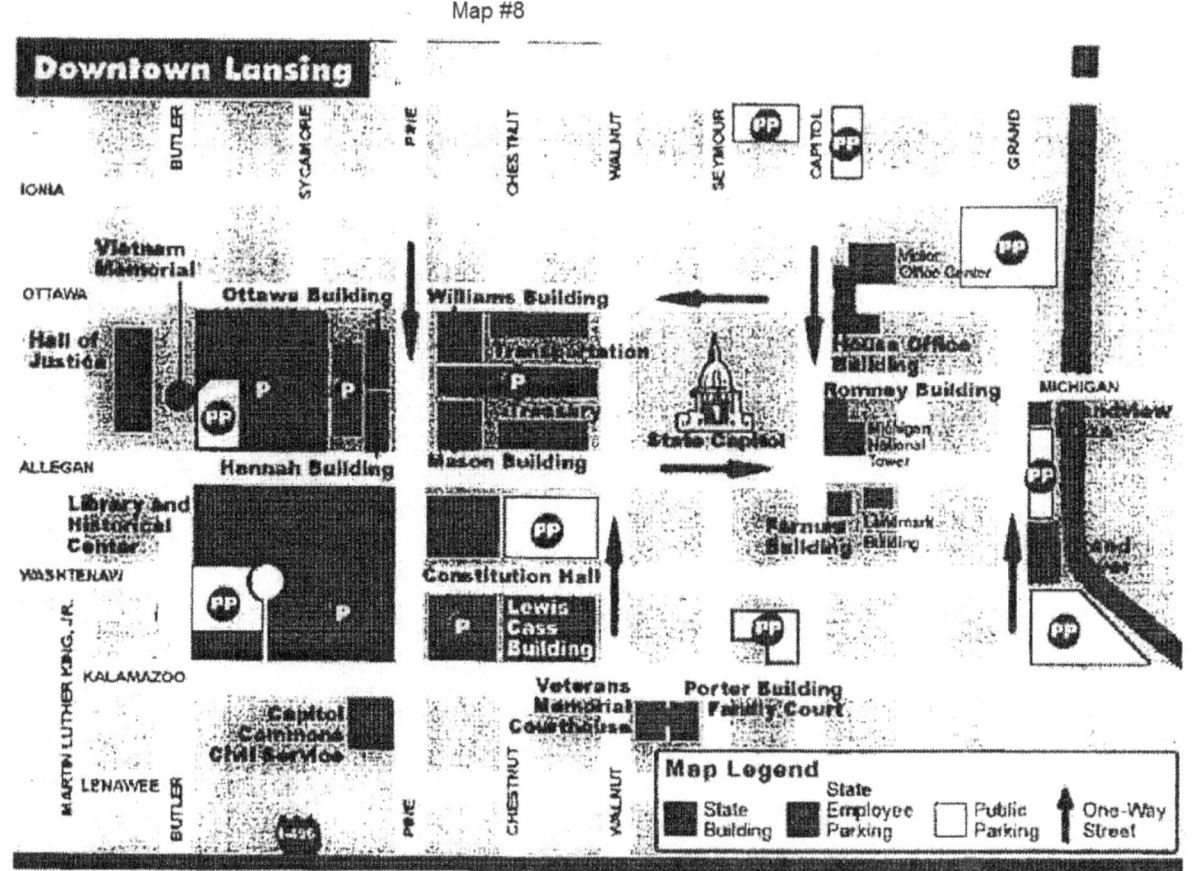

10. The SHORTEST legal way from the Library and Historical Center to Grandview Plaza is
    A. south on Butler, east on Kalamazoo, north on Grand
    B. east on Allegan, north on Grand
    C. north on Butler, east on Ionia, south on Grand
    D. north on Martin Luther King, Jr., east on Ottawa, south on Pine, east on Allegan, north on Grand

11. The SHORTEST legal way from the Victor Office Center to the Mason Building is
    A. west on Ottawa, south on Pine
    B. south on Capitol, west on Allegan, north on Pine
    C. south on Capitol, west on Washtenaw, north on Walnut, west on Allegan
    D. west on Ottawa, north on Seymour, west on Ionia, south on Pine

12. The SHORTESST legal way from the Treasury to the Hall of Justice is
    A. north on Walnut, west on Ottawa, south on Martin Luther King, Jr.
    B. west on Allegan
    C. east on Allegan, north on Grand, west on Ottawa, south on Martin Luther King. Jr.
    D. south on Walnut, west on Kalamazoo, north on Martin Luther King, Jr.

5 (#2)

13. The SHORTEST legal way from the Veterans Memorial Courthouse to the   13.____
    House Office Building is
    A. north on Walnut, east on Ottawa
    B. east on Kalamazoo, north on Capitol
    C. east on Kalamazoo, north on Grand, west on Ottawa
    D. north on Walnut, east on Allegan, north on Capitol

14. The SHORTEST legal way from Grand Tower to Constitution Hall is   14.____
    A. west on Washtenaw
    B. north on Grand, west on Allegan, south on Pine
    C. north on Grand, west on Ottaway, south on Pine
    D. south on Grand, west on Kalamazoo, north on Pine

Questions 15-19.

DIRECTIONS: Questions 15 through 19 refer to Figure #8, on the following page, and
              measure your ability to understand written descriptions of events. Each
              question presents a description of an accident or event and asks you which of
              the five drawings in Figure #8 BEST represents it.

              In the drawings, the following symbols are used:

              Moving Vehicle: ⌂   Non-moving Vehicle: ▮

              Pedestrian or Bicyclist: ●

              The path and direction of travel of a vehicle or pedestrian is indicated by a solid
              line.

              The path and direction of travel of each vehicle or pedestrian directly involved
              in a collision from the point of impact is indicated by a dotted line.

              In the space at the right, print the letter of the drawing that BEST fits the
              descriptions written below:

15. A driver headed west on Holly runs a red light and turns left. He sideswipes   15.____
    a car headed south in the intersection, and then flees south on Bay. The
    southbound car is diverted into the rear end of a car parked in the southbound
    lane on Bay.

16. A driver headed east on Holly runs a red light. Another driver headed south   16.____
    through the intersection slams on her brakes just in time to avoid a serious
    collision. The eastbound driver glances off the front of the southbound car and
    continues east, where he collides with a car parked in the eastbound lane on
    Holly.

17. A driver headed east on Holly runs a red light. She strikes the left front of a   17.____
    westbound car that is turning left from Holly onto Bay, and then veers left and
    strikes the rear end of a car parked in the northbound lane on Bay.

65

6 (#2)

18. A driver headed north on Bay strikes the right front of a car heading south in the intersection of Bay and Holly. After the collision, the driver veers left and collides with the rear end of a car parked in the westbound lane of Holly. The southbound car veers left and collides with the rear end of a car in the eastbound lane on Holly.

18.____

19. A driver headed north on Bay strikes the left front of a car heading south in the intersection of Bay and Holly. After the collision, the driver continues north and collides with the rear end of a car parked in the northbound lane. The southbound car continues south and collides with the rear end of a car in the southbound lane.

19.____

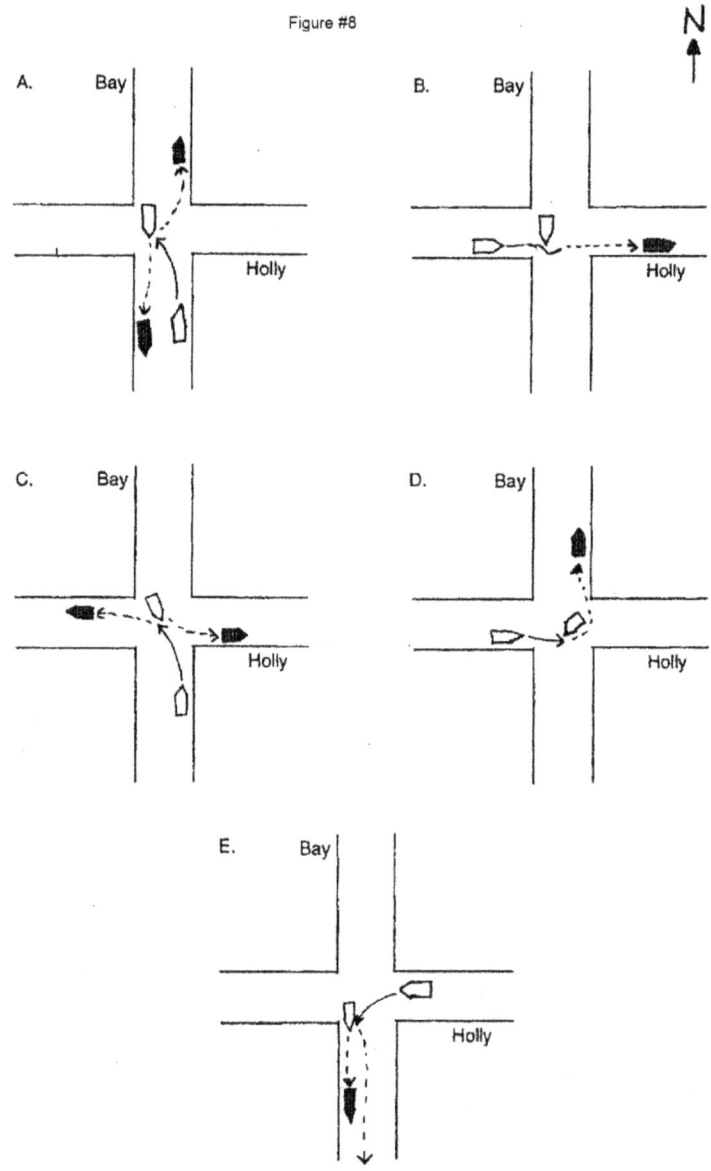

Figure #8

Questions 20-22.

DIRECTIONS: In Questions 20 through 22, choose the word or phrase CLOSEST in meaning to the word or phrase printed in capital letters.

20. LIABLE
    A. sensitive   B. dishonest   C. responsible   D. valid

    20.____

21. CLAIM
    A. debt   B. period   C. denial   D. banishment

    21.____

22. ADMISSIBLE
    A. false   B. conclusive   C. acceptable   D. indsputable

    22.____

Questions 23-25.

DIRECTIONS: Questions 22 through 25 measure your ability to do fieldwork-related arithmetic. Each question presents a separate arithmetic problem for you to solve.

23. Three departments divide an $800 payment. Department 1 takes $270, and Department 2 takes $150 more than Department 3.
    How much does Department 2 take?
    A. $150   B. $190   C. $340   D. $490

    23.____

24. Detective Smalley cleared 100 murder cases in five years. Each year he cleared six more than he cleared in the previous year.
    How many cases did he clear during the first year?
    A. 6   B. 8   C. 12   D. 18

    24.____

25. The purchasing agent bought three binders for $2 each, four reams of copier paper for $3 each and five packs of black pens for $7 each.
    How much did the agent spend?
    A. $12.00   B. $25.20   C. $53.00   D. $72.00

    25.____

KEY (CORRECT ANSWERS)

1. B
2. C
3. B
4. D
5. C

6. B
7. D
8. A
9. B
10. B

11. A
12. A
13. C
14. A
15. E

16. B
17. D
18. C
19. A
20. C

21. A
22. C
23. C
24. B
25. C

SOLUTIONS (QUESTIONS 1-9)

P implies Q = original statement

Not Q implies not P = contrapositive of the original statement. A statement and its contrapositive are logically equivalent.

Q implies P = converse of the original statement.

Not P implies not Q = inverse of the original statement. The converse and inverse of an original statement are logically equivalent.

P implies Q = Not P or Q

1. CORRECT ANSWER: B
   For Item I, we can conclude that it is Wednesday if and only if the garbage is collected. For Item II, the phrase "nobody has no" is equivalent to everybody has at least one."

2. CORRECT ANSWER: C
   For Item I, each statement is the converse of the other. Thus, they are not equivalent. For Item II, each statement says that each member of the Duluth Five is immune from prosecution.

3. CORRECT ANSWER: B
   For Item I, accepting a promotion is a necessary and sufficient condition for receiving a 10% raise. For Item II, we have the P implies Q condition, where P = hydraulic lines are flushed and Q = it is an inspection day.

4. CORRECT ANSWER: D
   For Item I, each statement is the converse of the other (so they are not equivalent). For Item II, the first statement simply states that a particular raven is black. The second statement says that all black birds are ravens. They are not equivalent.

5. CORRECT ANSWER: C
   The two scenarios are (a) a Rotary Club member is a subset of the set of all retirees, which is a subset of all planning commission member or (b) a Rotary Club member is a subset of all planning commission members, which is a subset of all retirees.

6. CORRECT ANSWER: B
   We know that some SWAT sniper members have poor aim. If we also know that all snipers on the SWAT team also have 20/20 vision, then we conclude that any sniper (including those with the worst aim) must have 20/20 vision.

7. CORRECT ANSWER: D
   The only way that Garson will not hear voices is if he takes his medication. The premature conclusion can only be correct if he takes his medication every Friday. None of choices A, B, or C mentions this specifically.

8. CORRECT ANSWER: A
If Frank is not the tallest and Jean is not the tallest, then the conclusion that Lily is the tallest is correct. This is a reasonable conclusion, unless all three are the same height (very unlikely).

9. CORRECT ANSWER: B
We are given that Dr. Lyons went to the cafeteria for lunch and that he did not have dessert. If Dr. Lyons always eats dessert when it is served in the cafeteria, we can conclude that the cafeteria did not serve dessert.

EXAMINATION SECTION
TEST 1

DIRECTIONS: Each question or incomplete statement is followed by several suggested answers or completions. Select the one that BEST answers the question or completes the statement. *PRINT THE LETTER OF THE CORRECT ANSWER IN THE SPACE AT THE RIGHT.*

1. Professional staff members in large organizations are sometimes frustrated by a lack of vital work-related information because of the failure of some middle-management supervisors to pass along unrestricted information from top management.
   All of the following are considered to be reasons for such failure to pass along information EXCEPT the supervisors'
   A. belief that information affecting procedures will be ignored unless they are present to supervise their subordinates
   B. fear that specific information will require explanation or justification
   C. inclination to regard the possession of information as a symbol of higher status
   D. tendency to treat information a private property

   1.____

2. Increasingly in government, employees' records are being handled by automated data processing systems. However, employees frequently doubt a computer's ability to handle their records properly.
   Which of the following is the BEST way for management to overcome such doubts?
   A. Conduct a public relations campaign to explain the savings certain to result from the use of computers
   B. Use automated data processing equipment made by the firm which has the best repair facilities in the industry
   C. Maintain a clerical force to spot check on the accuracy of the computer's recordkeeping
   D. Establish automated data processing systems that are objective, impartial, and take into account individual factors as far as possible

   2.____

3. Some management experts question the usefulness of offering cash to individual employees for their suggestions.
   Which of the following reasons for opposing cash awards is MOST valid?
   A. Emphasis on individual gain deters cooperative effort.
   B. Money spent on evaluating suggestions may outweigh the value of the suggestions.
   C. Awards encourage employees to think about unusual methods of doing work.
   D. Suggestions too technical for ordinary evaluation are usually presented.

   3.____

4. The use of outside consultants, rather than regular staff, in studying and recommending improvements in the operations of public agencies has been criticized.
   Of the following, the BEST argument in favor of using regular staff is that such staff can better perform the work because they
   A. are more knowledgeable about operations and problems
   B. can more easily be organized into teams consisting of technical specialists
   C. may wish to gain additional professional experience
   D. will provide reports which will be more interesting to the public since they are more experienced

5. One approach to organizational problem-solving is to have all problem-solving authority centralized at the top of the organization.
   However, from the viewpoint of providing maximum service to the public, this practice is UNWISE chiefly because it
   A. reduces the responsibility of the decision-makers
   B. produces delays
   C. reduces internal communications
   D. requires specialists

6. Research has shown that problem-solving efficiency is optimal when the motivation of the problem-solver is at a moderate rather than an extreme level.
   Of the following, probably the CHIEF reason for this is that the problem-solver
   A. will cause confusion among his subordinates when his motivation is too high
   B. must avoid alternate solutions that tend to lead him up blind alleys
   C. can devote his attention to both the immediate problem as well as to other relevant problems in the general area
   D. must feel the need to solve the problem but not so urgently as to direct all his attention to the need and none to the means of solution

7. Don't be afraid to make mistakes. Many organizations are paralyzed from the fear of making mistakes. As a result, they don't do the things they should; they don't try new and different ideas.
   For the effective supervisor, the MOST valid implication of this statement is that
   A. mistakes should not be encouraged, but there are some unavoidable risks in decision-making
   B. mistakes which stem from trying new and different ideas are usually not serious
   C. the possibility of doing things wrong is limited by one's organizational position
   D. the fear of making mistakes will prevent future errors

8. The duties of an employee under your supervision may be either routine, problem-solving, innovative, or creative.
   Which of the following BEST describes duties which are both innovative and creative?

A. Checking to make sure that work is done properly
B. Applying principles in a practical matter
C. Developing new and better methods of meeting goals
D. Working at two or more jobs at the same time

9. According to modern management theory, a supervisor who uses as little authority as possible and as much as is necessary would be considered to be using a mode that is
   A. autocratic
   B. inappropriate
   C. participative
   D. directive

10. Delegation involves establishing and maintaining effective working arrangements between a supervisor and the persons who report to him.
    Delegation is MOST likely to have taken place when the
    A. entire staff openly discusses common problems in order to reach solutions satisfactory to the supervisor
    B. performance of specified work is entrusted to a capable person, and the expected results are mutually understood
    C. persons assigned to properly accomplish work are carefully evaluated and given a chance to explain shortcomings
    D. supervisor provides specific written instructions in order to prevent anxiety on the part of inexperienced persons

11. Supervisors often not aware of the effect that their behavior has on their subordinates.
    The one of the following training methods which would be BEST for changing such supervisory behavior is _____ training.
    A. essential skills
    B. off-the-job
    C. sensitivity
    D. developmental

12. A supervisor, in his role as a trainer, may have to decide on the length and frequency of training sessions.
    When the material to be taught is new, difficult, and lengthy, the trainer should be guided by the principle that for BEST results in such circumstances, sessions should be
    A. longer, relatively fewer in number, and held on successive days
    B. shorter, relatively greater in number, and spaced at intervals of several days
    C. of average length, relatively fewer in number, and held at intermittent intervals
    D. of random length and frequency, but spaced at fixed intervals

13. Employee training which is based on realistic simulation, sometimes known as *game play* or *role play*, is sometimes preferable to learning from actual experience on the job.
    Which of the following is NOT a correct statement concerning the value of simulation to trainees?

A. Simulation allows for practice in decision-making without any need for subsequent discussion.
B. Simulation is intrinsically motivating because it offers a variety of challenges.
C. Compared to other, more traditional training techniques, simulation is dynamic.
D. The simulation environment is nonpunitive as compared to real life.

14. Programmed instruction as a method of training has all of the following advantages EXCEPT:
    A. Learning is accomplished in an optimum sequence of distinct steps.
    B. Trainees have wide latitude in deciding what is to be learned within each program.
    C. The trainee takes an active part in the learning process.
    D. The trainee receives immediate knowledge of the results of his response.

15. In a work-study program, trainees were required to submit weekly written performance reports in order to insure that work assignments fulfilled the program objectives.
    Such reports would also assist the administrator of the work-study program PRIMARILY to
    A. eliminate personal counseling for the trainees
    B. identify problems requiring prompt resolution
    C. reduce the amount of clerical work for all concerned
    D. estimate the rate at which budgeted funds are being expended

16. Which of the following would be MOST useful in order to avoid misunderstanding when preparing correspondence or reports?
    A. Use vocabulary which is at an elementary level
    B. Present each sentence as an individual paragraph
    C. Have someone other than the writer read the material for clarity
    D. Use general words which are open to interpretation

17. Which of the following supervisory methods would be MOST likely to train subordinates to give a prompt response to memoranda in an organizational setting where most transactions are informal?
    A. Issue a written directive setting forth a schedule of strict deadlines
    B. Let it be known, informally, that those who respond promptly will be rewarded
    C. Follow up each memorandum by a personal inquiry regarding the receiver's reaction to it
    D. Direct subordinates to furnish a precise explanation for ignoring memos

18. Conferences may fail for a number of reasons. Still, a conference that is an apparent failure may have some benefit.
    Which of the following would LEAST likely be such a benefit?
    It may
    A. increase for most participants their possessiveness about information they have

B. produce a climate of good will and trust among many of the participants
C. provide most participants with an opportunity to learn things about the others
D. serve as a unifying force to keep most of the individuals functioning as a group

19. Assume that you have been assigned to study and suggest improvements in an operating unit of a delegate agency whose staff has become overwhelmed with problems, has had inadequate resources, and has become accustomed to things getting worse. The staff is indifferent to cooperating with you because they see no hope of improvement.
Which of the following steps would be LEAST useful in carrying out your assignment?
    A. Encourage the entire staff to make suggestions to you for change
    B. Inform the staff that management is somewhat dissatisfied with their performance
    C. Let staff know that you are fully aware of their problems and stresses
    D. Look for those problem area where changes can be made quickly

19.____

20. Which of the following statements about employer-employee relations is NOT considered to be correct by leading managerial experts?
    A. An important factor in good employer-employee relations is treating workers respectfully.
    B. Employer-employee relations are profoundly influenced by the fundamentals of human nature.
    C. Good employer-employee relations must stem from top management and reach downward.
    D. Employee unions are usually a major obstacle to establishing good employer-employee relations.

20.____

21. In connection with labor relations, the term *management rights* GENERALLY refers to
    A. a managerial review system in a grievance system
    B. statutory prohibitions that bar monetary negotiations
    C. the impact of collective bargaining on government
    D. those subjects which management considers to be non-negotiable

21.____

22. Barriers may exist to the utilization of women in higher level positions. Some of these barriers are attitudinal in nature.
Which of the following is MOST clearly attitudinal in nature?
    A. Advancement opportunities which are vertical in nature and thus require seniority
    B. Experience which is inadequate or irrelevant to the needs of a dynamic and progressive organization
    C. Inadequate means of early identification of employees with talent and potential for advancement
    D. Lack of self-confidence on the part of some women concerning their ability to handle a higher position

22.____

23. Because a reader reacts to the meaning he associates with a word, we can neve be sure what emotional impact a word may carry or how it may affect our readers.
    The MOST logical implication of this statement for employees who correspond with members of the public is that
    A. a writer should try to select a neutral word that will not bias his writing by its hidden emotional meaning
    B. simple language should be used in writing letters denying requests so that readers are not upset by the denial
    C. every writer should adopt a writing style which he finds natural and easy
    D. whenever there is doubt as to how a word is defined, the dictionary should be consulted

    23.____

24. A public information program should be based on clear information about the nature of actual public knowledge and opinion. One way of learning about the views of the public is through the use of questionnaires.
    Which of the following is of LEAST importance in designing a questionnaire?
    A. A respondent should be asked for his name and address.
    B. A respondent should be asked to choose from among several statements the one which expresses his views.
    C. Questions should ask for responses in a form suitable for processing.
    D. Questions should be stated in familiar language.

    24.____

25. Assume that you have accepted an invitation to speak before an interested group about a problem. You have brought with you for distribution a number of booklets and other informational material.
    Of the following, which would be the BEST way to use this material?
    A. Distribute it before you begin talking so that the audience may read it at their leisure.
    B. Distribute it during your talk to increase the likelihood that it will be read.
    C. Hold it until the end of your talk, then announce that those who wish may take or examine the material.
    D. Before starting the talk, leave it on a table in the back of the room so that people may pick it up as they enter.

    25.____

KEY (CORRECT ANSWERS)

1. A
2. D
3. A
4. A
5. B

6. D
7. A
8. C
9. C
10. B

11. C
12. B
13. A
14. B
15. B

16. C
17. C
18. A
19. B
20. D

21. D
22. D
23. A
24. A
25. C

TEST 2

DIRECTIONS: Each question or incomplete statement is followed by several suggested answers or completions. Select the one that BEST answers the question or completes the statement. *PRINT THE LETTER OF THE CORRECT ANSWER IN THE SPACE AT THE RIGHT.*

1. Of the following, the FIRST step in planning an operation is to
    A. obtain relevant information
    B. identify the goal to be achieved
    C. consider possible alternatives
    D. make necessary assignments

2. A supervisor who is extremely busy performing routine tasks is MOST likely making INCORRECT use of what basic principle of supervision?
    A. Homogeneous Assignment
    B. Span of Control
    C. Work Distribution
    D. Delegation of Authority

3. Controls help supervisors to obtain information from which they can determine whether their staffs are achieving planned goals.
   Which one of the following would be LEAST useful as a control device?
    A. Employee diaries
    B. Organization charts
    C. Periodic inspections
    D. Progress charts

4. A certain employee has difficulty in effectively performing a particular portion of his routine assignments, but his overall productivity is average.
   As the direct supervisor of his individual, your BEST course of action would be to
    A. attempt to develop the man's capacity to execute the problematic facets of his assignments
    B. diversify the employee's work assignments in order to build up his confidence
    C. reassign the man to less difficult tasks
    D. request in a private conversation that the employee improve his work output

5. A supervisor who uses persuasion as a means of supervising a unit would GENERALLY also use which of the following practices to supervise his unit?
    A. Supervise and control the staff with an authoritative attitude to indicate that he is a *take-charge* individual
    B. Make significant changes in the organizational operations so as to improve job efficiency
    C. Remove major communication barriers between himself, subordinates, and management
    D. Supervise everyday operations while being mindful of the problems of his subordinates

6. Whenever a supervisor in charge of a unit delegate a routine task to a capable subordinate, he tells him exactly how to do it.

This practice is GENERALLY
- A. *desirable*, chiefly because good supervisors should be aware of the traits of their subordinates and delegate responsibilities to them accordingly
- B. *undesirable*, chiefly because only non-routine tasks should be delegated
- C. *desirable*, chiefly because a supervisor should frequently test the willingness of his subordinates to perform ordinary tasks
- D. *undesirable*, chiefly because a capable subordinate should usually be allowed to exercise his own discretion in doing a routine job

7. The one of the following activities through which a supervisor BEST demonstrates leadership ability is by
    - A. arranging periodic staff meetings in order to keep his subordinates informed about professional developments in the field
    - B. frequently issuing definite orders and directives which will lessen the need for subordinates to make decisions in handling any tasks assigned to them
    - C. devoting the major part of his time to supervising subordinates so as to simulate continuous improvement
    - D. setting aside time for self-development and research so as to improve the skills, techniques, and procedures of his unit

8. The following three statements relate to the supervision of employees:
    - I. The assignment of difficult tasks that offer a challenge is more conducive to good morale than the assignment of easy tasks.
    - II. The same general principles of supervision that apply to men are equally applicable to women.
    - III. The best retraining program should cover all phases of an employee's work in a general manner.

    Which of the following choices list ALL of the above statements that are generally correct?
    A. II, III   B. I   C. I, II   D. I, II, III

9. Which of the following examples BEST illustrates the application of the *exception principle* as a supervisory technique?
    - A. A complex job is divided among several employees who work simultaneously to complete the whole job in a shorter time.
    - B. An employee is required to complete any task delegated to him to such an extent that nothing is left for the superior who delegated the task except to approve it.
    - C. A superior delegates responsibility to a subordinate but retains authority to make the final decisions.
    - D. A superior delegates all work possible to his subordinates and retains that which requires his personal attention or performance

10. Assume that you are a supervisor. Your immediate superior frequently gives orders to your subordinates without your knowledge.
    Of the following, the MOST direct and effective way for you to handle this problem is to

A. tell our subordinates to take orders only from you
B. submit a report to higher authority in which you cite specific instances
C. discuss it with your immediate superior
D. find out to what extent your authority and prestige as a supervisor have been affected

11. In an agency which has as its primary purpose the protection of the public against fraudulent business practices, which of the following would GENERALLY be considered an *auxiliary* or *staff* rather than a *line* function?

    A. Interviewing victims of frauds and advising them about their legal remedies
    B. Daily activities directed toward prevention of fraudulent business practices
    C. Keeping records and statistics about business violations reported and corrected
    D. Follow-up inspections by investigators after corrective action has been taken

11.____

12. A supervisor can MOST effectively reduce the spread of false rumors through the *grapevine* by

    A. identifying and disciplining any subordinate responsible for initiating such rumors
    B. keeping his subordinates informed as much as possible about matters affecting them
    C. denying false rumors which might tend to lower staff morale and productivity
    D. making sure confidential matters are kept secure from access by unauthorized employees

12.____

13. A supervisor has tried to learn about the background, education, and family relationships of his subordinates through observation, personal contact, and inspection of their personnel records.
    These supervisor actions are GENERALLY

    A. *inadvisable*, chiefly because they may lead to charges of favoritism
    B. *advisable*, chiefly because they may make him more popular with his subordinates
    C. *inadvisable*, chiefly because his efforts may be regarded as an invasion of privacy
    D. *advisable*, chiefly because the information may enable him to develop better understanding of each of his subordinates

13.____

14. In an emergency situation, when action must be taken immediately, it is BEST for the supervisor to give orders in the form of

    A. direct commands which are brief and precise
    B. requests, so that his subordinates will not become alarmed
    C. suggestions which offer alternative courses of action
    D. implied directives, so that his subordinates may use their judgment in carrying them out

14.____

15. When demonstrating a new and complex procedure to a group of subordinates, it is ESSENTIAL that a supervisor
    A. go slowly and repeat the steps involved at least once
    B. show the employees common errors and the consequences of such errors
    C. go through the process at the usual speed so that the employees can see the rate at which they should work
    D. distribute summaries of the procedure during the demonstration and instruct his subordinates to refer to them afterwards

16. After a procedures manual has been written and distributed,
    A. continuous maintenance work is necessary to keep the manual current
    B. it is best to issue new manuals rather than make changes in the original manual
    C. no changes should be necessary
    D. only major changes should be considered

17. Of the following, the MOST important criterion of effective report writing is
    A. eloquence of writing style
    B. the use of technical language
    C. to be brief and to the point
    D. to cover all details

18. The use of electronic data processing
    A. has proven unsuccessful in most organizations
    B. has unquestionable advantages for all organizations
    C. is unnecessary in most organizations
    D. should be decided upon only after careful feasibility studies by individual organizations

19. The PRIMARY purpose of work measurement is to
    A. design and install a wage incentive program
    B. determine who should be promoted
    C. establish a yardstick to determine extent of progress
    D. set up a spirit of competition among employee

20. The action which is MOST effective in gaining acceptance of a study by the agency which is being studied is
    A. a directive from the agency head to install a study based on recommendations included in a report
    B. a lecture-type presentation following approval of the procedure
    C. a written procedure in narrative form covering the proposed system with visual presentations and discussions
    D. procedural charts showing the *before* situation, forms, steps, etc., to the employees affected

5 (#2)

21. Which organization principle is MOST closely related to procedural analysis and improvement?
    A. Duplication, overlapping, and conflict should be eliminated.
    B. Managerial authority should be clearly defined.
    C. The objectives of the organization should be clearly defined.
    D. Top management should be freed of burdensome detail.

21._____

22. Which one of the following is the MAJOR objective of operational audits?
    A. Detecting fraud
    B. Determining organization problems
    C. Determining the number of personnel needed
    D. Recommending opportunities for improving operating and management practices

22._____

23. Of the following, the formalization of organization structure is BEST achieved by
    A. a narrative description of the plan of organization
    B. functional charts
    C. job descriptions together with organization charts
    D. multi-flow charts

23._____

24. Budget planning is MOST useful when it achieves
    A. cost control
    B. forecast of receipts
    C. performance review
    D. personnel reduction

24._____

25. GENERALLY, in applying the principle of delegation in dealing with subordinates, a supervisor
    A. allows his subordinates to set up work goals and to fix the limits within which they can work
    B. allows his subordinates to set up work goals and then gives detailed orders as to how they are to be achieved
    C. makes relatively few decisions by himself and frames his orders in broad, general terms
    D. provides externalized motivation for his subordinate

25._____

KEY (CORRECT ANSWERS)

1. B
2. D
3. B
4. A
5. D

6. D
7. C
8. C
9. D
10. C

11. C
12. B
13. D
14. A
15. A

16. A
17. C
18. D
19. C
20. C

21. A
22. D
23. C
24. A
25. C

READING COMPREHENSION
UNDERSTANDING AND INTERPRETING WRITTEN MATERIAL
EXAMINATION SECTION
TEST 1

DIRECTIONS: Each question or incomplete statement is followed by several suggested answers or completions. Select the one that BEST answers the question or completes the statement. *PRINT THE LETTER OF THE CORRECT ANSWER IN THE SPACE AT THE RIGHT.*

Questions 1-2.

DIRECTIONS: Questions 1 and 2 are to be answered SOLELY on the basis of the information given in the following paragraph.

It is argued by some that the locale of the trial should be given little or no consideration. Facts are facts, they say, and if presented properly to a jury panel they will be productive of the same results regardless of where the trial is held. However, experience shows great differences in the methods of handling claims by juries. In some counties, large demands in personal injury suits are viewed with suspicion by the jury. In others, the jurors are liberal in dealing with someone else's funds.

1. According to the above paragraph, it would be ADVISABLE for an examiner on a personal injury case to

    A. get information as to the kind of verdicts that are usually awarded by juries in the county of trial
    B. give little or no consideration to the locale of the trial
    C. look for incomplete and improper presentation of facts to the jury if the verdict was not justified by the facts
    D. offer a high but realistic initial settlement figure so that no temptation is left to the claimant to gamble on the jury's verdict

2. According to the above statement, the argument that the location of a trial in a personal injury suit CANNOT counteract the weight of the evidence is

    A. basically sound
    B. disproven by the differences in awards for similar claims
    C. substantiated in those cases where the facts are properly and carefully presented to the injury
    D. supported by experience which shows great differences in the methods of handling claims by juries

Questions 3-6.

DIRECTIONS: Questions 3 through 6 are to be answered SOLELY on the basis of the following excerpt from a recorded annual report of the police department. This material should be read first and then referred to in answering these questions.

LEGAL BUREAU

One of the more important functions of this bureau is to analyze and furnish the department with pertinent information concerning Federal and State statutes and local laws which affect the department, law enforcement or crime prevention. In addition, all measure introduced in the State Legislature and the City Council which may affect this department are carefully reviewed by members of the Legal Bureau and, where necessary, opinions and recommendations thereon are prepared.

Another important function of this office is the prosecution of cases in the Criminal Courts. This is accomplished by assignment of attorneys who are members of the Legal Bureau to appear in those cases which are deemed to raise issues of importance to the department or questions of law which require technical presentation to facilitate proper determination; and also in those cases where request is made for such appearances by a judge or magistrate, some other official of the city, or a member of the force.

Proposed legislation was prepared and sponsored for introduction in the State Legislature and, at this writing, one of these proposals has already been enacted into law and five others are presently on the Governor's desk awaiting executive action. The new law prohibits the sale or possession of a hypodermic syringe or needle by an unauthorized person. The bureau's proposals awaiting executive action pertain to an amendment to the Criminal Procedure Law prohibiting desk officers from taking bail in gambling cases or in cases mentioned in the Criminal Procedure Law, including confidence men and swindlers as jostlers in the Penal Law; prohibiting the sale of switchblade knives of any size to children under 16 and bills extending the licensing period of gunsmiths.

The Legal Bureau has regularly cooperated with the Corporation Counsel and the District Attorneys in respect to matters affecting this department, and has continued to advise and represent the Police Athletic League, the Police Sports Association, the Police Relief Fund, and the Police Pension Fund.

3. Members of the Legal Bureau frequently appear in Criminal Court for the purpose of

    A. defending members of the Police Force
    B. raising issues of important to the Police Department
    C. prosecuting all offenders arrested by members of the Force
    D. facilitating proper determination of questions of law requiring technical presentation

4. The Legal Bureau sponsored a bill that would

    A. extend the licenses of gunsmiths
    B. prohibit the sale of switchblade knives to children of any size
    C. place confidence men and swindlers in the same category as jostlers in the Penal Law
    D. prohibit desk officers from admitting gamblers, confidence men, and swindlers to bail

5. One of the functions of the Legal Bureau is to

   A. review and make recommendations on proposed Federal laws affecting law enforcement
   B. prepare opinions on all measures introduced in the State Legislature and the City Council
   C. furnish the Police Department with pertinent information concerning all new Federal and State laws
   D. analyze all laws affecting the work of the Police Department

6. The one of the following that is NOT a function of the Legal Bureau is

   A. law enforcement and crime prevention
   B. prosecution of all cases in Women's Court
   C. advise and represent the Police Sports Association
   D. lecturing at the Police Academy

7. It is usual in public service for recruits to serve a probationary period before they receive tenured positions. The objective of this is to observe them in actual service, to teach them the duties of their position, and to provide a means for eliminating those who prove they are not suited for this kind of work. During this period, firings may be made at the discretion of the chief.
   Which one of the following is BEST supported by the above selection?

   A. Demonstrated fitness for the job is the basis for retention of probationary employees.
   B. Trial appointments protect the appointee from unfair dismissal practices.
   C. Public service employees need experience and instruction before permanent appointment.
   D. Exams must be given to determine the ability of probationary employees.

8. As the fundamental changes sought to be brought about in the inmates of a correctional institution can be accomplished only under good leadership, it follows that the quality of the staff whose duty it is to influence and guide the inmates in the right direction is more important than the physical facilities of the institution.
   Of the following, the MOST accurate conclusion based on the preceding statement is that

   A. the development of leadership is the fundamental change brought about in inmates by good quality staff
   B. the physical facilities of an institution are not very important in bringing about fundamental changes in the inmates
   C. with proper training the entire staff of a correctional institution can be developed into good leaders
   D. without good leadership the basic changes desired in the inmates of a correctional institution cannot be brought about

Questions 9-11.

DIRECTIONS: Questions 9 through 11 are to be answered SOLELY on the basis of the following paragraph.

The law enforcement agency is one of the most important agencies in the field of juvenile delinquency prevention. This is so not because of the social work connected with this problem, however, for this is not a police matter, but because the officers are usually the first to come in contact with the delinquent. The manner of arrest and detention makes a deep impression upon him and affects his life-long attitude toward society and the law. The juvenile court is perhaps the most important agency in this work. Contrary to the general opinion, however, it is not primarily concerned with putting children into correctional schools. The main purpose of the juvenile court is to save the child and to develop his emotional make-up in order that he can grow up to be a decent and well-balanced citizen. The system of probation is the means whereby the court seeks to accomplish these goals.

9. According to this paragraph, police work is an important part of a program to prevent juvenile delinquency because

   A. social work is no longer considered important in juvenile delinquency prevention
   B. police officers are the first to have contact with the delinquent
   C. police officers jail the offender in order to be able to change his attitude toward society and the law
   D. it is the first step in placing the delinquent in jail

10. According to this paragraph, the CHIEF purpose of the juvenile court is to

    A. punish the child for his offense
    B. select a suitable correctional school for the delinquent
    C. use available means to help the delinquent become a better person
    D. provide psychiatric care for the delinquent

11. According to this paragraph, the juvenile court directs the development of delinquents under its care CHIEFLY by

    A. placing the child under probation
    B. sending the child to a correctional school
    C. keeping the delinquent in prison
    D. returning the child to his home

Questions 12-14.

DIRECTIONS: Questions 12 through 14 are to be answered on the basis of the following paragraph.

An assassination is an act that consists of a plotted, attempted or actual murder of a prominent political figure by an individual who performs this act in other than a governmental role. This definition draws a distinction between political execution and assassination. An execution may be regarded as a political killing, but it is initiated by the organs of the state, while an assassination can always be characterized as an illegal act. A prominent figure must be the target of the killing, since the killing of lesser members of the political community is included within a wider category of internal political turmoil, namely, terrorism. Assassination is also to be distinguished from homicide. The target of the aggressive act must be a political figure rather than a private person. The killing of a prime minister by a member of an insurrectionist or underground group clearly qualifies as an assassination. So does an act by a deranged individual who tries to kill not just any individual, but the individual in his political role - as President, for example.

12. Assume that a nationally prominent political figure is charged with treason by the state, tried in a court of law, found guilty, and hanged by the state. According to the above passage, it would be MOST appropriate to regard his death as a(n)   12.____

    A. assassination   B. execution
    C. aggressive act   D. homicide

13. According to the above passage, which of the following statements is CORRECT?   13.____

    A. The assassination of a political figure is an illegal act.
    B. A private person may be the target of an assassination attempt.
    C. The killing of an obscure member of a political community is considered an assassination event.
    D. An execution may not be regarded as a political killing.

14. Of the following, the MOST appropriate title for this passage would be   14.____

    A. ASSASSINATION - LEGAL ASPECTS
    B. POLITICAL CAUSES OF ASSASSINATION
    C. ASSASSINATION - A DEFINITION
    D. CATEGORIES OF ASSASSINATION

Questions 15-17.

DIRECTIONS: Questions 15 through 17 are to be answered SOLELY on the basis of the following paragraph.

All applicants for an original license to operate a catering establishment shall be fingerprinted. This shall include the officers, employees, and stockholders of the company and the members of a partnership. In case of a change, by addition or substitution, occurring during the existence of a license, the person added or substituted shall be fingerprinted. However, in the case of a hotel containing more than 200 rooms, only the officer or manager filing the application is required to be fingerprinted. The police commissioner may also, at his discretion, exempt the employees and stockholders of any company. The fingerprints shall be taken on one copy of Form C.E. 20 and on two copies of C.E. 21. One copy of Form C.E. 21 shall accompany the application. Fingerprints are not required with a renewal application.

15. According to the above paragraph, an employee added to the payroll of a licensed catering establishment which is not in a hotel must be fingerprinted   15.____

    A. always
    B. unless he has been previously fingerprinted for another license
    C. unless exempted by the police commissioner
    D. only if he is the manager or an officer of the company

16. According to the above paragraph, it would be MOST accurate to state that   16.____

    A. Form C.E. 20 must accompany a renewal application
    B. Form C.E. 21 must accompany all applications
    C. Form C.E. 21 must accompany an original application
    D. both Forms C.E. 20 and C.E. 21 must accompany all applications

17. A hotel of 270 rooms has applied for a license to operate a catering establishment on the premises.
According to the instructions for fingerprinting given in the above paragraph, the _____ shall be fingerprinted.

    A. officers, employees, and stockholders
    B. officers and the manager
    C. employees
    D. officer filing the application

17.____

Questions 18-24.

DIRECTIONS: Read the following two paragraphs. Then answer the questions by selecting the answer
    A - if the paragraphs indicate it is TRUE
    B - if the paragraphs indicate it is PROBABLY true
    C - if the paragraphs indicate it is PROBABLY false
    D - if the paragraphs indicate it is FALSE

    The fallacy underlying what some might call the eighteenth and nineteenth century misconceptions of the nature of scientific investigations seems to lie in a mistaken analogy. Those who said they were investigating the structure of the universe imagined themselves as the equivalent of the early explorers and map makers. The explorers of the fifteenth and sixteenth centuries had opened up new worlds with the aid of imperfect maps; in their accounts of distant lands, there had been some false and many ambiguous statements. But by the time everyone came to believe the world was round, the maps of distant continents were beginning to assume a fairly consistent pattern. By the seventeenth century, methods of measuring space and time had laid the foundations for an accurate geography.

    On this basic issue there is far from complete agreement among philosophers *of* science today. You can, each of you, choose your side and find highly distinguished advocates for the point of view you have selected. However, in view of the revolution in physics, anyone who now asserts that science is an exploration of the universe must be prepared to shoulder a heavy burden of proof. To my mind, the analogy between the map maker and the scientist is false. A scientific theory is not even the first approximation to a map; it is not a need; it is a policy -- an economical and fruitful guide to action, by scientific investigators.

18. The author thinks that 18th and 19th century science followed the same technique as the 15th century geographers.

18.____

19. The author disagrees with the philosophers who are labelled realists.

19.____

20. The author believes there is a permanent structure to the universe.

20.____

21. A scientific theory is an economical guide to exploring what cannot be known absolutely.

21.____

22. Philosophers of science accept the relativity implications of recent research in physics.

22.____

23. It is a matter of time and effort before modern scientists will be as successful as the geographers.

23.____

24. The author believes in an indeterminate universe.

24.____

25. Borough X reports that its police force makes fewer arrests per thousand persons than any of the other boroughs.
From this statement, it is MOST probable that

    A. sufficient information has not been given to warrant any conclusion
    B. the police force of Borough X is less efficient
    C. fewer crimes are being committed in Borough X
    D. fewer crimes are being reported in Borough X

KEY (CORRECT ANSWERS)

1.	A	11.	A
2.	B	12.	B
3.	D	13.	A
4.	C	14.	C
5.	D	15.	C
6.	A	16.	C
7.	A	17.	D
8.	D	18.	D
9.	B	19.	B
10.	C	20.	D

21. A
22. D
23. D
24. B
25. A

TEST 2

DIRECTIONS: Each question or incomplete statement is followed by several suggested answers or completions. Select the one that BEST answers the question or completes the statement. *PRINT THE LETTER OF THE CORRECT ANSWER IN THE SPACE AT THE RIGHT.*

Questions 1-2.

DIRECTIONS: Questions 1 and 2 are to be answered on the basis of the information given in the following passage.

Assume that a certain agency is having a problem at one of its work locations because a sizable portion of the staff at that location is regularly tardy in reporting to work. The management of the agency is primarily concerned about eliminating the problem and is not yet too concerned about taking any disciplinary action. An investigator is assigned to investigate to determine, if possible, what might be causing this problem.

After several interviews, the investigator sees that low morale created by poor supervision at this location is at least part of the problem. In addition, there is a problem of tardiness and lack of interest.

1. Given the goals of the investigation and assuming that the investigator was using a non-directive approach in this interview, of the following, the investigator's MOST effective response should be:

    A. You know, you are building a bad record of tardiness
    B. Can you tell me more about this situation?
    C. What kind of person is your superior?
    D. Do you think you are acting fairly towards the agency by being late so often?

2. Given the goals of the investigation and assuming the investigator was using a directed approach in this interview, of the following, the investigator's response should be:

    A. That doesn't seem like much of an excuse to me
    B. What do you mean by saying that you've lost interest?
    C. What problems are there with the supervision you are getting?
    D. How do you think your tardiness looks in your personnel record?

Questions 3-5.

DIRECTIONS: Questions 3 through 5 are to be answered SOLELY on the basis of the following passage.

As investigators, we are more concerned with the utilitarian than the philosophical aspects of ethics and ethical standards, procedures, and conduct. As a working consideration, we might view ethics as the science of doing the right thing at the right time in the right manner in conformity with the normal, everyday standards imposed by society; and in conformity with the judgment society would be expected to make concerning the rightness or wrongness of what we have done.

An ethical code might be considered a basic set of rules and regulations to which we must conform in the performance of investigative duties. Ethical standards, procedures, and conduct might be considered the logical workings of our ethical code in its everyday application to our work. Ethics also necessarily involves morals and morality. We must eventually answer the self-imposed question of whether or not we have acted in the right way in conducting our investigative activities in their individual and total aspects.

3. Of the following, the MOST suitable title for the above passage is 3.____

   A. THE IMPORTANCE OF RULES FOR INVESTIGATORS
   B. THE BASIC PHILOSOPHY OF A LAWFUL SOCIETY
   C. SCIENTIFIC ASPECTS OF INVESTIGATIONS
   D. ETHICAL GUIDELINES FOR THE CONDUCT OF INVESTIGATIONS

4. According to the above passage, ethical considerations for investigators involve 4.____

   A. special standards that are different from those which apply to the rest of society
   B. practices and procedures which cannot be evaluated by others
   C. individual judgments by investigators of the appropriateness of their own actions
   D. regulations which are based primarily upon a philosophical approach

5. Of the following, the author's PRINCIPAL purpose in writing the above passage seems to have been to 5.____

   A. emphasize the importance of self-criticism in investigative activities
   B. explain the relationship that exists between ethics and investigative conduct
   C. reduce the amount of unethical conduct in the area of investigations
   D. seek recognition by his fellow investigators for his academic treatment of the subject matter

Questions 6-8.

DIRECTIONS: Questions 6 through 8 are to be answered SOLELY on the basis of the following passage.

The investigator must remember that acts of omission can be as effective as acts of commission in affecting the determination of disputed issues. Acts of omission, such as failure to obtain available information or failure to verify dubious information, manifest themselves in miscarriages of justice and erroneous adjudications. An incomplete investigation is an erroneous investigation because a conclusion predicated upon inadequate facts is based on quicksand.

When an investigator throws up his hands and admits defeat, the reason for this action does not necessarily lie in his possible laziness and ineptitude. It is more likely that the investigator has made his conclusions after exhausting only those avenues of investigation of which he is aware. He has exercised good faith in his belief that nothing else can be done.

This tendency must be overcome by all investigators if they are to operate at top efficiency. If no suggestion for new or additional action can be found in any authority, an investigator should use his own initiative to cope with a given situation. No investigator should ever hesitate to set precedents. It is far better in the final analysis to attempt difficult solutions, even if the chances of error are obviously present, than it is to take refuge in the spineless adage: If you don't do anything, you don't do it wrong.

6. Of the following, the MOST suitable title for the above passage is 6.____
   A. THE NEED FOR RESOURCEFULNESS IN INVESTIGATIONS
   B. PROCEDURES FOR COMPLETING AN INVESTIGATION
   C. THE DEVELOPMENT OF STANDARDS FOR INVESTIGATORS
   D. THE CAUSES OF INCOMPLETE INVESTIGATIONS

7. Of the following, the author of this passage considers that the LEAST important consideration in developing new investigative methods is 7.____
   A. efficiency   B. caution
   C. imagination   D. thoroughness

8. According to this passage, which of the following statements is INCORRECT? 8.____
   A. Lack of creativity may lead to erroneous investigations.
   B. Acts of omission are sometimes as harmful as acts of commission.
   C. Some investigators who give up on a case are lazy or inept.
   D. An investigator who gives up on a case is usually not acting in good faith.

Questions 9-12.

DIRECTIONS: Questions 9 through 12 are to be answered on the basis of the following paragraph.

A report of investigation should not be weighed down by a mass of information which is hardly material or only remotely relevant, or which fails to prove a point, clarify an issue, or aid the inquiry even by indirection. Some investigative agencies, however, value the report for its own sake, considering it primarily as a justification of the investigative activity contained therein. Every step is listed to show that no logical measure has been overlooked and to demonstrate that the reporting agent is beyond criticism. This system serves to provide reviewing authorities with a ready means of checking subordinates and provides order, method, and routine to investigative activity. In addition, it may offer supervisors and investigators a sense of security; the investigator would know within fairly exact limits what is expected of him and the supervisor may be comforted by the knowledge that his organization may not be reasonably criticized in a particular case on the grounds of obvious omissions or inertia. To the state's attorney and others, however, who must take administrative action on the basis of the report, the irrelevant and immaterial information thwarts the purpose of the investigation by dimming the issues and obscuring the facts that are truly contributory to the proof.

9. From the point of view of the supervising investigator, a drawback of having the investigator prepare the type of report which the state's attorney would like is that it 9.____
   A. gives a biased and one-sided view of what should have been an impartial investigation
   B. has only limited usefulness as an indication that all proper investigative methods were used by the investigator
   C. overlooks logical measures, removing the responsibility for taking those measures which the investigator should otherwise have been expected to take
   D. sets fairly exact limits to what the supervisor can expect of the investigator

10. District attorneys do not like reports of investigations in which every step is listed because

   A. their administrative action is then based on irrelevant and immaterial information
   B. it places the investigator beyond criticism, making the responsibility of the district attorney that much greater
   C. of the difficulty of finding among the mass of information the portion which is meaningful and useful
   D. the inclusion of indirect or hardly material information is not in accord with the order in which the steps were taken

11. As expressed in the above paragraph, the type of report which MOST investigators prefer to prepare is

   A. a step-by-step account of their activities, including both fruitful and unfruitful steps, since to do so provides order and method and gives them a sense of security
   B. not made clear, even though current practice in some agencies is to include every step taken in the investigation
   C. one from which useless and confusing information has been excluded because it is not helpful and is poor practice
   D. one not weighed down by a mass of irrelevant information but one which shows within fairly exact limits what was expected of them

12. With regard to the type of information which an investigator should include in his report, the above paragraph expresses the opinion that

   A. it is best to include in the report only that information which supports the conclusions of the investigator
   B. reports should include all relevant and clarifying information and exclude information on inquiries which had no productive result
   C. reports should include sufficient information to demonstrate that the investigator has been properly attending to his duties and all the information which contributes toward proof of what occurred in the case
   D. the most logical thing to do is to list every step in the investigation and its result

Questions 13-17.

DIRECTIONS: Questions 13 through 17 are to be answered SOLELY on the basis of the following paragraph.

Those statutes of limitations which are of interest to a claim examiner are the ones affecting third party actions brought against an insured covered by a liability policy of insurance. Such statutes of limitations are legislative enactments limiting the time within which such actions at law may be brought. Research shows that such periods differ from state to state and vary within the states with the type of action brought. The laws of the jurisdiction in which the action is brought govern and determine the period within which the action may be instituted, regardless of the place of the cause of action or the residence of the parties at the time of cause of action. The period of time set by a statute of limitations for a tort action starts from the moment the alleged tort is committed. The period usually extends continuously until its expiration, upon which legal action may no longer be brought. However, there is a suspension of the running of the period when a defendant has concealed himself in order to avoid service of legal process. The suspension continues until the defendant discontinues his concealment and then the period starts running again. A defendant may, by his agreement or conduct, be legally barred from asserting the statute of limitations as a defense to an action. The insurance carrier for the defendant may, by the misrepresentation of the claims man, cause such a bar against use of the statute of limitations by the defendant. If the claim examiner of the insurance carrier has by his conduct or assertion lulled the plaintiff into a false sense of security by false representations, the defendant may be barred from setting up the statute of limitations as a defense.

13. Of the following, the MOST suitable title for the above paragraph is

    A. FRAUDULENT USE OF THE STATUTE OF LIMITATIONS
    B. PARTIES AT INTEREST IN A LAWSUIT
    C. THE CLAIM EXAMINER AND THE LAW
    D. THE STATUTE OF LIMITATIONS IN CLAIMS WORK

14. The period of time during which a third party action may be brought against an insured covered by a liability policy depends on

    A. the laws of the jurisdiction in which the action is brought
    B. where the cause of action which is the subject of the suit took place
    C. where the claimant lived at the time of the cause of action
    D. where the insured lived at the time of the cause of action

15. Time limits in third party actions which are set by the statutes of limitations described above are

    A. determined by claimant's place of residence at start of action
    B. different in a state for different actions
    C. the same from state to state for the same type of action
    D. the same within a state regardless of type of action

16. According to the above paragraph, grounds which may be legally used to prevent a defendant from using the statute of limitations as a defense in the action described are

    A. defendant's agreement or concealment; a charge of liability for death and injury
    B. defendant's agreement or conduct; misrepresentation by the claims man
    C. fraudulent concealment by claim examiner; a charge of liability for death or injury; defendant's agreement
    D. misrepresentation by claim examiner of carrier; defendant's agreement; plaintiff's concealment

17. Suppose an alleged tort was commited on January 1, 2008 and that the period in which action may be taken is set at three years by the statute of limitations. Suppose further that the defendant, in order to avoid service of legal process, had concealed himself from July 1, 2010 through December 31, 2010.
In this case, the defendant may not use the statute of limitations as a defense unless action is brought by the plaintiff after _____, 2011.

    A. January 1   B. February 28
    C. June 30   D. August 1

Questions 18-20.

DIRECTIONS: Questions 18 through 20 are to be answered SOLELY on the basis of information contained in the following passage.

No matter how well the interrogator adjusts himself to the witness and how precisely he induces the witness to describe his observations, mistakes still can be made. The mistakes made by an experienced interrogator may be comparatively few, but as far as the witness is concerned, his path is full of pitfalls. Modern *witness psychology* has shown that even the most honest and trustworthy witnesses are apt to make grave mistakes in good faith. It is, therefore, necessary that the interrogator get an idea of the weak links in the testimony in order to check up on them in the event that something appears to be strange or not quite satisfactory.

Unfortunately, modern witness psychology does not yet offer any means of directly testing the credibility of testimony. It lacks precision and method, in spite of worthwhile attempts on the part of learned men. At the same time, witness psychology, through the gathering of many experiences concerning the weaknesses of human testimony, has been of invaluable service. It shows clearly that only evidence of a technical nature has absolute value as proof.

Testimony may be separated into the following stages: (1) perception, (2) observation, (3) mind fixation of the observed occurrences, in which fantasy, association of ideas, and personal judgment participate, and (4) expression in oral or written form, where the testimony is transferred from one witness to another or to the interrogator.

Each of these stages offers innumerable possibilities for the distortion of testimony.

18. The above passage indicates that having witnesses talk to each other before testifying is a practice which is GENERALLY

    A. *desirable,* since the witnesses will be able to correct each other's errors in observation before testimony
    B. *undesirable,* since the witnesses will collaborate on one story to tell the investigator
    C. *undesirable,* since one witness may distort his testimony because of what another witness may erroneously say
    D. *desirable,* since witnesses will become aware of discrepancies in their own testimony and can point out the discrepancies to the investigator

19. According to the above passage, the one of the following which would be the MOST reliable for use as evidence would be the testimony of a

    A. handwriting expert about a signature on a forged check
    B. trained police officer about the identity of a criminal
    C. laboratory technician about an accident he has observed
    D. psychologist who has interviewed any witnesses who relate conflicting stories

20. Concerning the validity of evidence, it is CLEAR from the above passage that

    A. only evidence of a technical nature is at all valuable
    B. the testimony of witnesses is so flawed that it is usually valueless

C. an investigator, by knowing modern witness psychology, will usually be able to perceive mistaken testimony
D. an investigator ought to expect mistakes in even the most reliable witness testimony

Questions 21-22.

DIRECTIONS: Questions 21 and 22 are to be answered SOLELY on the basis of the information contained in the passage below. This passage represents a report prepared by a subordinate superior concerning a school demonstration.

On April 1, a group of students, each holding an anti-apartheid sign, was involved in a demonstration on the grounds of Columbia University. The students began by locking the main entrance doors to the Administration Building and preventing faculty and students from entering or leaving the building.

The C.O. of the police detail at the scene requested additional assistance of four female detectives, an Emergency Service van, and a police photographer equipped with a Polaroid instamatic camera.

When the additional assistance arrived, the Commanding Officer directed the students to disperse. His justification for the order was that the demonstrators were violating the rights of other students and certain faculty members by denying them access to the Administration Building. The students ignored the order to disperse and the Commanding Officer of the police detail ordered them to be removed.

Another group of students who had been standing in front of the library were sympathetic toward the demonstrators and charged the police. Several police officers were injured during the ensuing hostilities.

Eventually, order was restored. That evening, the television coverage presented a neutral and fairly accurate account of the incident.

21. Which of the following statements MOST clearly and accurately reflects the contents of the report?

    A. A large group of students, all of whom were holding anti-apartheid signs, was involved in a demonstration on the grounds of Columbia University.
    B. A large group of students, some of whom were holding anti-apartheid signs, was involved in a demonstration on the grounds of Columbia University.
    C. Each of a group of Columbia students carrying anti-apartheid signs was involved in a demonstration on the grounds of Columbia University.
    D. Each of the students involved in the demonstration on the grounds of Columbia University was holding an anti-apartheid sign.

22. Which of the following statements MOST clearly and accurately reflects the contents of the report?

A. The Commanding Officer of the police detail justified his order that the demonstrators disperse when the additional assistance arrived.
B. When the additional assistance arrived, the Commanding Officer of the police detail justified his order that the demonstrators disperse.
C. The Commanding Officer of the police detail directed the students to disperse when the additional assistance arrived.
D. The Commanding Officer of the police detail requested additional assistance because the student demonstrators were violating the rights of other students and certain faculty members.

23. Which of the following statements MOST clearly and accurately reflects the contents of the report?

   A. Another group of students charged the police because they were sympathetic toward the police.
   B. The evening television coverage of the demonstration was fair and accurate.
   C. The group of students who had been standing in front of the library was sympathetic toward the demonstrators.
   D. Several police officers were injured during the hostilities which took place in front of the library.

Questions 24-25.

DIRECTIONS: Questions 24 and 25 are to be answered SOLELY on the basis of the information given in the following paragraph.

Credibility of a witness is usually governed by his character and is evidenced by his reputation for truthfulness. Personal or financial reasons or a criminal record may cause a witness to give false information to avoid being implicated. Age, sex, physical and mental abnormalities, loyalty, revenge, social and economic status, indulgence in alcohol, and the influence of other persons are some of the many factors which may affect the accuracy, willingness, or ability with which witnesses observe, interpret, and describe occurrences.

24. According to the above paragraph, a witness may, for personal reasons, give wrong information about an occurrence because he

   A. wants to protect his reputation for truthfulness
   B. wants to embarrass the investigator
   C. doesn't want to become involved
   D. doesn't really remember what happened

25. According to the above paragraph, factors which influence the witness of an occurrence may affect

   A. not only what he tells about it but what he was able and wanted to see of it
   B. only what he describes and interprets later but not what he actually sees at the time of the event
   C. what he sees but not what he describes
   D. what he is willing to see but not what he is able to see

KEY (CORRECT ANSWERS)

1.	B	11.	B
2.	C	12.	B
3.	D	13.	D
4.	C	14.	A
5.	B	15.	B
6.	A	16.	B
7.	B	17.	C
8.	D	18.	C
9.	B	19.	A
10.	C	20.	D

21. D
22. C
23. C
24. C
25. A

———

PREPARING WRITTEN MATERIAL

PARAGRAPH REARRANGEMENT
COMMENTARY

The sentences that follow are in scrambled order. You are to rearrange them in proper order and indicate the letter choice containing the correct answer at the space at the right.

Each group of sentences in this section is actually a paragraph presented in scrambled order. Each sentence in the group has a place in that paragraph; no sentence is to be left out. You are to read each group of sentences and decide upon the best order in which to put the sentences so as to form a well-organized paragraph.

The questions in this section measure the ability to solve a problem when all the facts relevant to its solution are not given.

More specifically, certain positions of responsibility and authority require the employee to discover connection between events sometimes, apparently, unrelated. In order to do this, the employee will find it necessary to correctly infer that unspecified events have probably occurred or are likely to occur. This ability becomes especially important when action must be taken on incomplete information.

Accordingly, these questions require competitors to choose among several suggested alternatives, each of which presents a different sequential arrangement of the events. Competitors must choose the MOST logical of the suggested sequences.

In order to do so, they may be required to draw on general knowledge to infer missing concepts or events that are essential to sequencing the given events. Competitors should be careful to infer only what is essential to the sequence. The plausibility of the wrong alternatives will always require the inclusion of unlikely events or of additional chains of events which are NOT essential to sequencing the given events.

It's very important to remember that you are looking for the best of the four possible choices, and that the best choice of all may not even be one of the answers you're given to choose from.

There is no one right way to solve these problems. Many people have found it helpful to first write out the order of the sentences, as they would have arranged them, on their scrap paper before looking at the possible answers. If their optimum answer is there, this can save them some time. If it isn't, this method can still give insight into solving the problem. Others find it most helpful to just go through each of the possible choices, contrasting each as they go along. You should use whatever method feels comfortable and works for you.

While most of these types of questions are not that difficult, we've added a higher percentage of the difficult type, just to give you more practice. Usually there are only one or two questions on this section that contain such subtle distinctions that you're unable to answer confidently. And you then may find yourself stuck deciding between two possible choices, neither of which you're sure about.

EXAMINATION SECTION

TEST 1

DIRECTIONS: Each question consists of several sentences which can be arranged in a logical sequence. For each question, select the choice which places the numbered sentences in the MOST logical sequence. *PRINT THE LETTER OF THE CORRECT ANSWER IN THE SPACE AT THE RIGHT.*

1. I. A body was found in the woods.
   II. A man proclaimed innocence.
   III. The owner of a gun was located.
   IV. A gun was traced.
   V. The owner of a gun was questioned.
   The CORRECT answer is:
   A. IV, III, V, II, I   B. II, I, IV, III, V   C. I, IV, III, V, II
   D. I, III, V, II, IV   E. I, II, IV, III, V

   1.____

2. I. A man is in a hunting accident.
   II. A man fell down a flight of steps.
   III. A man lost his vision in one eye,
   IV. A man broke his leg.
   V. A man had to walk with a cane.
   The CORRECT answer is:
   A. II, IV, V, I, III   B. IV, V, I, III, II   C. III, I, IV, V, II
   D. I, III, V, II, IV   E. I, III, II, IV, V

   2.____

3. I. A man is offered a new job.
   II. A woman is offered a new job.
   III. A man works as a waiter.
   IV. A woman works as a waitress.
   V. A woman gives notice.
   The CORRECT answer is:
   A. IV, II, V, III, I   B. IV, II, V, I, III   C. II, IV, V, III, I
   D. III, I, IV, II, V   E. IV, III, II, V, I

   3.____

4. I. A train let the station late.
   II. A man was late for work.
   III. A man lost his job.
   IV. Many people complained because the train was late.
   V. There was a traffic jam.
   The CORRECT answer is:
   A. V, II, I, IV, III   B. V, I, IV, II, III   C. V, I, II, IV, III
   D. I, V, IV, II, III   E. II, I, IV, V, III

   4.____

103

5. I. The burden of proof as to each issue is determined before trial and remains upon the same party throughout the trial.
    II. The jury is at liberty to believe one witness' testimony as against a number of contradictory witnesses.
    III. In a civil case, the party bearing the burden of proof is required to prove his contention by a fair preponderance of the evidence.
    IV. However, it must be noted that a fair preponderance of evidence does not necessarily mean a greater number of witnesses.
    V. The burden of proof is the burden which rests upon one of the parties to an action to persuade the trier of the facts, generally the jury, that a proposition he asserts is true.
    VI. If the evidence is equally balanced, or if it leaves the jury in such doubt as to be unable to decide the controversy either way, judgment must be given against the party upon whom the burden of proof rests.
    The CORRECT answer is:
    A. III, II, V, IV, I, VI   B. I, II, VI, V, III, IV   C. III, IV, V, I, II, VI
    D. V, I, III, VI, IV, II   E. I, V, III, VI, IV, II

6. I. If a parent is without assets and is unemployed, he cannot be convicted of the crime of non-support of a child.
    II. The term *sufficient ability* has been held to mean sufficient financial ability.
    III. It does not matter if his unemployment is by choice or unavoidable circumstances.
    IV. If he fails to take any steps at all, he may be liable to prosecution for endangering the welfare of a child.
    V. Under the penal law, a parent is responsible for the support of his minor child only if the parent is of *sufficient ability*.
    VI. An indigent parent may meet his obligation by borrowing money or by seeking aid under the provisions of the Social Welfare Law.
    The CORRECT answer is:
    A. VI, I, V, III, II, IV   B. I, III, V, II, IV, VI   C. V, II, I, III, VI, IV
    D. I, VI, IV, V, II, III   E. II, V, I, III, VI, IV

7. I. Consider, for example, the case of a rabble rouser who urges a group of twenty people to go out and break the windows of a nearby factory.
    II. Therefore, the law fills the indicated gap with the crime of *inciting to riot*.
    III. A person is considered guilty of inciting to riot when he urges ten or more persons to engage in tumultuous and violent conduct of a kind likely to create public alarm.
    IV. However, if he has not obtained the cooperation of at least four people, he cannot be charged with unlawful assembly.
    V. The charge of inciting to riot was added to the law to cover types of conduct which cannot be classified as either the crime of *riot* or the crime of *unlawful assembly*.
    VI. If he acquires the acquiescence of at least four of them, he is guilty of unlawful assembly even if the project does not materialize.
    The CORRECT answer is:
    A. III, V, I, VI, IV, II   B. V, I, IV, VI, II, III   C. III, IV, I, V, II, VI
    D. V, I, IV, VI, III, II   E. V, III, I, VI, IV, II

8. I. If, however, the rebuttal evidence presents an issue of credibility, it is for the jury to determine whether the presumption has, in fact, been destroyed.
    II. Once sufficient evidence to the contrary is introduced, the presumption disappears from the trial.
    III. The effect of a presumption is to place the burden upon the adversary to come forward with evidence to rebut the presumption.
    IV. When a presumption is overcome and ceases to exist in the case, the fact or facts which gave rise to the presumption still remain.
    V. Whether a presumption has been overcome is ordinarily a question for the court.
    VI. Such information may furnish a basis for a logical inference.
    The CORRECT answer is:
    A. IV, VI, II, V, I, III   B. III, II, V, I, IV, VI   C. V, III, VI, IV, II, I
    D. V, IV, I, II, VI, III   E. II, III, V, I, IV, VI

8.____

9. I. An executive may answer a letter by writing his reply on the face of the letter itself instead of having a return letter typed.
    II. This procedure is efficient because it saves the executive's time, the typist's time, and saves office file space.
    III. Copying machines are used in small offices as well as large offices to save time and money in making brief replies to business letters.
    IV. A copy is made on a copying machine to go into the company files, while the original is mailed back to the sender.
    The CORRECT answer is:
    A. I, II, IV, III   B. I, IV, II, III   C. III, I, IV, II   D. III, IV, II, I

9.____

10. I. Most organizations favor one of the types but always include the others to a lesser degree.
    II. However, we can detect a definite trend toward greater use of symbolic control.
    III. We suggest that our local police agencies are today primarily utilizing material control.
    IV. Control can be classified into three types: physical, material, and symbolic.
    The CORRECT answer is:
    A. IV, II, III, I   B. II, I, IV, III   C. III, IV, II, I   D. IV, I, III, II

10.____

11. I. Project residents had first claim to this use, followed by surrounding neighborhood children.
    II. By contrast, recreation space within the project's interior was found to be used more often by both groups.
    III. Studies of the use of project grounds in many cities showed grounds left open for public use were neglected and unused, both by residents and by members of the surrounding community.
    IV. Project residents had clearly laid claim to the play spaces, setting up and enforcing unwritten rules for use.
    V. Each group, by experience, found their activities easily disrupted by other groups, and their claim to the use of space for recreation difficult to enforce.

11.____

4 (#1)

The CORRECT answer is:
A. IV, V, I, II, III
B. V, II, IV, III, I
C. I, IV, III, II, V
D. III, V, II, IV, I

12. I. They do not consider the problems correctable within the existing subsidy formula and social policy of accepting all eligible applicants regardless of social behavior.
    II. A recent survey, however, indicated that tenants believe these problems correctable by local housing authorities and management within the existing financial formula.
    III. Many of the problems and complaints concerning public housing management and design have created resentment between the tenant and the landlord.
    IV. This same survey indicated that administrators and managers do not agree with the tenants.
    The CORRECT answer is:
    A. II, I, III, IV   B. I, III, IV, II   C. III, II, IV, I   D. IV, II, I, III

13. I. In single-family residences, there is usually enough distance between tenants to prevent occupants from annoying one another.
    II. For example, a certain small percentage of tenant families has one or more members addicted to alcohol.
    III. While managers believe in the right of individuals to live as they choose, the manager becomes concerned when the pattern of living jeopardizes others' rights.
    IV. Still others turn night into day, staging lusty entertainments which carry on into the hours when most tenants are trying to sleep.
    V. In apartment buildings, however, tenants live so closely together that any misbehavior can result in unpleasant living conditions.
    VI. Other families engage in violent argument.
    The CORRECT answer is:
    A. III, II, V, IV, VI, I
    B. I, V, II, VI, IV, III
    C. II, V, IV, I, III, VI
    D. IV, II, V, VI, III, I

14. I. Congress made the commitment explicit in the Housing Act of 194, establishing as a national goal the realization of a *decent home and suitable environment for every American family*.
    II. The result has been that the goal of decent home and suitable environment is still as far distant as ever for the disadvantaged urban family.
    III. In spite of this action by Congress, federal housing programs have continued to be fragmented and grossly underfunded.
    IV. The passage of the National Housing Act signaled a few federal commitment to provide housing for the nation's citizens.
    The CORRECT answer is:
    A. I, IV, III, II   B. IV, I, III, II   C. IV, I, II, III   D. II, IV, I, III

15. I. The greater expense does not necessarily involve *exploitation*, but it is often perceived as exploitative and unfair by those who are aware of the price differences involved, but unaware of operating costs.
II. Ghetto residents believe they are *exploited* by local merchants, and evidence substantiates some of these beliefs.
III. However, stores in low-income areas were more likely to be small independents, which could not achieve the economies available to supermarket chains and were, therefore, more likely to charge higher prices, and the customers were more likely to buy smaller-sized packages which are more expensive per unit of measure.
IV. A study conducted in one city showed that distinctly higher prices were charged for goods sold in ghetto stores in other areas.
The CORRECT answer is:
  A. IV, II, I, III   B. IV, I, III, II   C. II, IV, III, I   D. II, III, IV, I

15.____

KEY (CORRECT ANSWERS)

1.	C	6.	C	11.	D
2.	E	7.	A	12.	C
3.	B	8.	B	13.	B
4.	B	9.	C	14.	B
5.	D	10.	D	15.	C

PREPARING WRITTEN MATERIAL
EXAMINATION SECTION
TEST 1

Questions 1-15.

DIRECTIONS: For each of Questions 1 through 15, select from the options given below the MOST applicable choice, and mark your answer accordingly.
    A. The sentence is correct.
    B. The sentence contains a spelling error only.
    C. The sentence contains an English grammar error only.
    D. The sentence contains both a spelling error and an English grammar error.

1. He is a very dependible person whom we expect will be an asset to this division.   1.____

2. An investigator often finds it necessary to be very diplomatic when conducting an interview.   2.____

3. Accurate detail is especially important if court action results from an investigation.   3.____

4. The report was signed by him and I since we conducted the investigation jointly.   4.____

5. Upon receipt of the complaint, an inquiry was begun.   5.____

6. An employee has to organize his time so that he can handle his workload efficiantly.   6.____

7. It was not apparent that anyone was living at the address given by the client.   7.____

8. According to regulations, there is to be at least three attempts made to locate the client.   8.____

9. Neither the inmate nor the correction officer was willing to sign a formal statement.   9.____

10. It is our opinion that one of the persons interviewed were lying.   10.____

11. We interviewed both clients and departmental personel in the course of this investigation.   11.____

12. It is concievable that further research might produce additional evidence.   12.____

13. There are too many occurences of this nature to ignore.   13.____

14. We cannot accede to the candidate's request. 14.____

15. The submission of overdue reports is the reason that there was a delay in completion of this investigation. 15.____

Questions 16-25.

DIRECTIONS: Each of Questions 16 through 25 may be classified under one of the following four categories:
    A. Faulty because of incorrect grammar or sentence structure.
    B. Faulty because of incorrect punctuation.
    C. Faulty because of incorrect spelling.
    D. Correct

Examine each sentence carefully to determine under which of the above four options it is best classified. Then, in the space at the right, write the letter preceding the option which is the BEST of the four suggested above. Each incorrect sentence contains but one type of error. Consider a sentence to be correct if it contains none of the types of errors mentioned, even though there may be other correct ways of expressing the same thought.

16. Although the department's supply of scratch pads and stationary have diminished considerably, the allotment for our division has not been reduced. 16.____

17. You have not told us whom you wish to designate as your secretary. 17.____

18. Upon reading the minutes of the last meeting, the new proposal was taken up for consideration. 18.____

19. Before beginning the discussion, we locked the door as a precautionery measure. 19.____

20. The supervisor remarked, "Only those clerks, who perform routine work, are permitted to take a rest period." 20.____

21. Not only will this duplicating machine make accurate copies, but it will also produce a quantity of work equal to fifteen transcribing typists. 21.____

22. "Mr. Jones," said the supervisor, "we regret our inability to grant you an extention of your leave of absence. 22.____

23. Although the employees find the work monotonous and fatigueing, they rarely complain. 23.____

24. We completed the tabulation of the receipts on time despite the fact that Miss Smith our fastest operator was absent for over a week. 24.____

25. The reaction of the employees who attended the meeting, as well as the reaction of those who did not attend, indicates clearly that the schedule is satisfactory to everyone concerned.

25.____

KEY (CORRECT ANSWERS)

1.	D		11.	B
2.	A		12.	B
3.	A		13.	B
4.	C		14.	A
5.	A		15.	C
6.	B		16.	A
7.	B		17.	D
8.	C		18.	A
9.	A		19.	C
10.	C		20.	B

21. A
22. C
23. C
24. B
25. D

TEST 2

Questions 1-15.

DIRECTIONS: Questions 1 through 15 consist of two sentences. Some are correct according to ordinary formal English usage. Others are incorrect because they contain errors in English usage, spelling, or punctuation. Consider a sentence correct if it contains no errors in English usage, spelling, or punctuation, even if there may be other ways of writing the sentence correctly. Mark your answer:
- A. If only sentence I is correct.
- B. If only sentence II is correct.
- C. If sentences 1 and II are correct.
- D. If neither sentence I nor II is correct.

1. I. The influence of recruitment efficiency upon administrative standards is readily apparant.
    II. Rapid and accurate thinking are an essential quality of the police officer.

2. I. The administrator of a police department is constantly confronted by the demands of subordinates for increased personnel in their respective units.
    II. Since a chief executive must work within well-defined fiscal limits, he must weigh the relative importance of various requests.

3. I. The two men whom the police arrested for a parking violation were wanted for robbery in three states.
    II. Strong executive control from the top to the bottom of the enterprise is one of the basic principals of police administration.

4. I. When he gave testimony unfavorable to the defendant loyalty seemed to mean very little.
    II. Having run off the road while passing a car, the patrolman gave the driver a traffic ticket.

5. I. The judge ruled that the defendant's conversation with his doctor was a privileged communication.
    II. The importance of our training program is widely recognized; however, fiscal difficulties limit the program's effectiveness.

6. I. Despite an increase in patrol coverage, there were less arrests for crimes against property this year.
    II. The investigators could hardly have expected greater cooperation from the public.

7. I. Neither the patrolman nor the witness could identify the defendant as the driver of the car.
    II. Each of the officers in the class received their certificates at the completion of the course.

8.   I. The new commander made it clear that those kind of procedures would no longer be permitted.
    II. Giving some weight to performance records is more advisable than making promotions solely on the basis of test scores.
            8.____

9.   I. A deputy sheriff must ascertain whether the debtor, has any property.
    II. A good deputy sheriff does not cause histerical excitement when he executes a process.
            9.____

10.   I. Having learned that he has been assigned a judgment debtor, the deputy sheriff should call upon him.
    II. The deputy sheriff may seize and remove property without requiring a bond.
            10.____

11.   I. If legal procedures are not observed, the resulting contract is not enforseable.
    II. If the directions from the creditor's attorney are not in writing, the deputy sheriff should request a letter of instructions from the attorney.
            11.____

12.   I. The deputy sheriff may confer with the defendant and enter this defendants' place of business.
    II. A deputy sheriff must ascertain from the creditor's attorney whether the debtor has any property against which he may proceede.
            12.____

13.   I. The sheriff has a right to do whatever is necessary for the purpose of executing the order of the court.
    II. The written order of the court gives the sheriff general authority and he is governed in his acts by a very simple principal.
            13.____

14.   I. Either the patrolman or his sergeant are always ready to help the public.
    II. The sergeant asked the patrolman when he would finish the report.
            14.____

15.   I. The injured man could not hardly talk.
    II. Every officer had ought to had in their reports on time.
            15.____

Questions 16-26.

DIRECTIONS: For each of the sentences given below, numbered 16 through 25, select from the following choices the MOST correct choice and print your choice in the space at the right. Select as your answer:
    A. If the statement contains an unnecessary word or expression
    B. If the statement contains a slang term or expression ordinarily not acceptable in government report writing.
    C. If the statement contains an old-fashioned word or expression, where a concrete, plain term would be more useful.
    D. If the statement contains no major faults.

16. Every one of us should try harder.   16.____

17. Yours of the first instant has been received.   17.____

3 (#2)

18. We will have to do a real snow job on him. 18.____
19. I shall contact him next Thursday. 19.____
20. None of us were invited to the meeting with the community. 20.____
21. We got this here job to do. 21.____
22. She could not help but see the mistake in the checkbook. 22.____
23. Don't bug the Director about the report. 23.____
24. I beg to inform you that your letter has been received. 24.____
25. This project is all screwed up. 25.____

KEY (CORRECT ANSWERS)

1. D
2. C
3. A
4. D
5. B

6. B
7. A
8. D
9. D
10. C

11. B
12. D
13. A
14. D
15. D

16. D
17. C
18. B
19. D
20. D

21. B
22. D
23. B
24. C
25. B

TEST 3

DIRECTIONS: Questions 1 through 25 are sentences taken from reports. Some are correct according to ordinary English usage. Others are incorrect because they contain errors in English usage, spelling, or punctuation. Consider a sentence correct if it contains no errors in English usage, spelling, or punctuation, even if there may be other ways of writing the sentence correctly. Mark your answer:
- A. If only sentence I is correct
- B. If only sentence II is correct
- C. If sentences I and II are correct
- D. If neither sentence I nor II is correct

1.
   I. The Neighborhood Police Team Commander and Team Patrolmen are encouraged to give to the public the widest possible verbal and written disemination of information regarding the existence and purposes of the program.
   II. The police must be vitally interelated with every segment of the public they serve.

2.
   I. If social gambling, prostitution, and other vices are to be prohibited, the law makers should provide the manpower and method for enforcement.
   II. In addition to checking on possible crime locations such as hallways, roofs yards and other similar locations, Team Patrolmen are encouraged to make known their presence to members of the community.

3.
   I. The Neighborhood Police Team Commander is authorized to secure, the cooperation of local publications, as well as public and private agencies, to further the goals of the program.
   II. Recruitment from social minorities is essential to effective police work among minorities and meaningful relations with them.

4.
   I. The Neighborhood Police Team Commander and his men have the responsibility for providing patrol service within the sector territory on a twenty-four hour basis.
   II. While the patrolman was walking his beat at midnight he noticed that the clothing stores' door was partly open.

5.
   I. Authority is granted to the Neighborhood Police Team to device tactics for coping with the crime in the sector.
   II. Before leaving the scene of the accident, the patrolman drew a map showing the positions of the automobiles and indicated the time of the accident as 10 M. in the morning.

6.
   I. The Neighborhood Police Team Commander and his men must be kept apprised of conditions effecting their sector.
   II. Clear, continuous communication with every segment of the public served based on the realization of mutual need and founded on trust and confidence is the basis for effective law enforcement.

7. I. The irony is that the police are blamed for the laws they enforce when they are doing their duty.
    II. The Neighborhood Police Team Commander is authorized to prepare and distribute literature with pertinent information telling the public whom to contact for assistance.

7._____

8. I. The day is not far distant when major parts of the entire police compliment will need extensive college training or degrees.
    II. Although driving under the influence of alcohol is a specific charge in making arrests, drunkenness is basically a health and social problem.

8._____

9. I. If a deputy sheriff finds that property he has to attach is located on a ship, he should notify his supervisor.
    II. Any contract that tends to interfere with the administration of justice is illegal.

9._____

10. I. A mandate or official order of the court to the sheriff or other officer directs it to take into possession property of the judgment debtor.
    II. Tenancies from month-to-month, week-to-week, and sometimes year-to-year are termenable.

10._____

11. I. A civil arrest is an arrest pursuant to an order issued by a court in civil litigation.
    II. In a criminal arrest, a defendant is arrested for a crime he is alleged to have committed.

11._____

12. I. Having taken a defendant into custody, there is a complete restraint of personal liberty.
    II. Actual force is unnecessary when a deputy sheriff makes an arrest.

12._____

13. I. When a husband breaches a separation agreement by failing to supply to the wife the amount of money to be paid to her periodically under the agreement, the same legal steps may be taken to enforce his compliance as in any other breach of contract.
    II. Having obtained the writ of attachment, the plaintiff is then in the advantageous position of selling the very property that has been held for him by the sheriff while he was obtaining a judgment.

13._____

14. I. Being locked in his desk, the investigator felt sure that the records would be safe.
    II. The reason why the witness changed his statement was because he had been threatened.

14._____

15. I. The investigation had just began then an important witness disappeared.
    II. The check that had been missing was located and returned to its owner, Harry Morgan, a resident of Suffolk County, New York.

15._____

16. I. A supervisor will find that the establishment of standard procedures enables his staff to work more efficiently.
    II. An investigator hadn't ought to give any recommendations in his report if he is in doubt.

17. I. Neither the investigator nor his supervisor is ready to interview the witness.
    II. Interviewing has been and always will be an important asset in investigation.

18. I. One of the investigator's reports has been forwarded to the wrong person.
    II. The investigator stated that he was not familiar with those kind of cases.

19. I. Approaching the victim of the assault, two large bruises were noticed by me.
    II. The prisoner was arrested for assault, resisting arrest, and use of a deadly weapon.

20. I. A copy of the orders, which had been prepared by the captain, was given to each patrolman.
    II. It's always necessary to inform an arrested person of his constitutional rights before asking him any questions.

21. I. To prevent further bleeding, I applied a tourniquet to the wound.
    II. John Rano a senior officer was on duty at the time of the accident.

22. I. Limiting the term "property" to tangible property, in the criminal mischief setting, accords with prior case law holding that only tangible property came within the purview of the offense of malicious mischief.
    II. Thus, a person who intentionally destroys the property of another, but under an honest belief that he has title to such property, cannot be convicted of criminal mischief under the Revised Penal Law.

23. I. Very early in it's history, New York enacted statutes from time to time punishing, either as a felony or as a misdemeanor, malicious injuries to various kinds of property: piers, boos, dams, bridges, etc.
    II. The application of the statute is necessarily restricted to trespassory takings with larcenous intent: namely with intent permanently or virtually permanently to "appropriate" property or "deprive" the owner of its use.

24. I. Since the former Penal Law did not define the instruments of forgery in a general fashion, its crime of forgery was held to be narrower than the common law offense in this respect and to embrace only those instruments explicitly specified in the substantive provisions.
    II. After entering the barn through an open door for the purpose of stealing, it was closed by the defendants.

25. I. The use of fire or explosives to destroy tangible property is proscribed by the criminal mischief provisions of the Revised Penal Law.
    II. The defendant's taking of a taxicab for the immediate purpose of affecting his escape did not constitute grand larceny.

25._____

KEY (CORRECT ANSWERS)

1.	D	11.	C
2.	D	12.	B
3.	B	13.	C
4.	A	14.	D
5.	D	15.	B
6.	D	16.	A
7.	C	17.	C
8.	D	18.	A
9.	C	19.	B
10.	D	20.	C

21.	A
22.	C
23.	B
24.	A
25.	A

TEST 4

Questions 1-4.

DIRECTIONS: Each of the two sentences in Questions 1 through 4 may be correct or may contain errors in punctuation, capitalization, or grammar. Mark your answer:
- A. If there is an error only in sentence I
- B. If there is an error only in sentence II
- C. If there is an error in both sentences I and II
- D. If both sentences are correct.

1.
   I. It is very annoying to have a pencil sharpener, which is not in working order.
   II. Patrolman Blake checked the door of Joe's Restaurant and found that the lock has been jammed.

   1.____

2.
   I. When you are studying a good textbook is important.
   II. He said he would divide the money equally between you and me.

   2.____

3.
   I. Since he went on the city council a year ago, one of his primary concerns has been safety in the streets.
   II. After waiting in the doorway for about 15 minutes, a black sedan appeared.

   3.____

Questions 4-8.

DIRECTIONS: Each of the sentences in Questions 4 through 8 may be classified under one of the following four categories:
- A. Faulty because of incorrect grammar
- B. Faulty because of incorrect punctuation
- C. Faulty because of incorrect capitalization or incorrect spelling
- D. Correct

Examine each sentence carefully to determine under which of the above four options it is BEST classified. Then, in the space at the right, print the capitalized letter preceding the option which is the BEST of the four suggested above. Each faulty sentence contains but one type of error. Consider a sentence to be correct if it contains none of the types of errors mentioned, even though there may be other correct ways of expressing the same thought.

4. They told both he and I that the prisoner had escaped. 4.____

5. Any superior officer, who, disregards the just complaints of his subordinates, is remiss in the performance of his duty. 5.____

6. Only those members of the national organization who resided in the Middle west attended the conference in Chicago. 6.____

7. We told him to give the investigation assignment to whoever was available. 7.____

8. Please do not disappoint and embarass us by not appearing in court. 8.____

Questions 9-13

DIRECTIONS: Each of Questions 9 through 13 consists of three sentences lettered A, B, and C. In each of these questions, one of the sentences may contain an error in grammar, sentence structure, or punctuation, or all three sentences may be correct. If one of the sentence in a question contains an error in grammar, sentence structure, or punctuation, print in the space at the right the capital letter preceding the sentence which contains the error. If all three sentences are correct, print the letter D.

9.
   A. Mr. Smith appears to be less competent than I in performing these duties.
   B. The supervisor spoke to the employee, who had made the error, but did not reprimand him.
   C. When he found the book lying on the table, he immediately notified the owner.

   9.____

10.
    A. Being locked in the desk, we were certain that the papers would not be taken.
    B. It wasn't I who dictated the telegram; I believe it was Eleanor.
    C. You should interview whoever comes to the office today.

    10.____

11.
    A. The clerk was instructed to set the machine on the table before summoning the manager.
    B. He said that he was not familiar with those kind of activities.
    C. A box of pencils, in addition to erasers and blotters, was included in the shipment of supplies.

    11.____

12.
    A. The supervisor remarked, "Assigning an employee to the proper type of work is not always easy."
    B. The employer found that each of the applicants were qualified to perform the duties of the position.
    C. Any competent student is permitted to take this course if he obtains the consent of the instructor.

    12.____

13.
    A. The prize was awarded to the employee whom the judges believed to be most deserving.
    B. Since the instructor believes his book is the better of the two, he is recommending it for use in the school.
    C. It was obvious to the employees that the completion of the task by the scheduled date would require their working overtime.

    13.____

Questions 14-20.

DIRECTIONS: In answering Questions 14 through 20, choose the sentence which is BEST from the point of view of English usage suitable for a business report.

14. A. The client's receiving of public assistance checks at two different addresses were disclosed by the investigation.
    B. The investigation disclosed that the client was receiving public assistance checks at two different addresses.
    C. The client was found out by the investigation to be receiving public assistance checks at two different addresses.
    D. The client has been receiving public assistance checks at two different addresses, disclosed the investigation.

14.____

15. A. The investigation of complaints are usually handled by this unit, which deals with internal security problems in the department.
    B. This unit deals with internal security problems in the department usually investigating complaints.
    C. Investigating complaints is this unit's job, being that it handles internal security problems in the department.
    D. This unit deals with internal security problems in the department and usually investigates complaints.

15.____

16. A. The delay in completing this investigation was caused by difficulty in obtaining the required documents from the candidate.
    B. Because of difficulty in obtaining the required documents from the candidate is the reason that there was a delay in completing this investigation.
    C. Having had difficulty in obtaining the required documents from the candidate, there was a delay in completing this investigation.
    D. Difficulty in obtaining the required documents from the candidate had the affect of delaying the completion of this investigation.

16.____

17. A. This report, together with documents supporting our recommendation, are being submitted for your approval.
    B. Documents supporting our recommendation is being submitted with the report for your approval.
    C. This report, together with documents supporting our recommendation, is being submitted for your approval.
    D. The report and documents supporting our recommendation is being submitted for your approval.

17.____

18. A. The chairman himself, rather than his aides, has reviewed the report.
    B. The chairman himself, rather than his aides, have reviewed the report.
    C. The chairmen, not the aide, has reviewed the report.
    D. The aide, not the chairmen, have reviewed the report.

18.____

19. A. Various proposals were submitted but the decision is not been made.
    B. Various proposals has been submitted but the decision has not been made.
    C. Various proposals were submitted but the decision is not been made.
    D. Various proposals have been submitted but the decision has not been made.

19._____

20. A. Everyone were rewarded for his successful attempt.
    B. They were successful in their attempts and each of them was rewarded.
    C. Each of them are rewarded for their successful attempts.
    D. The reward for their successful attempts were made to each of them.

20._____

21. The following is a paragraph from a request for departmental recognition consisting of five numbered sentences submitted to a Captain for review. These sentences may or may not have errors in spelling, grammar, and punctuation:
    (1) The officers observed the subject Mills surreptitiously remove a wallet from the woman's handbag and entered his automobile. (2) As they approached Mills, he looked in their direction and drove away. (3) The officers pursued in their car. (4) Mills executed a series of complicated manuvers to evade the pursuing officers. (5) At the corner of Broome and Elizabeth Streets, Mills stopped the car, got out, raised his hands and surrendered to the officers. Which one of the following BEST classifies the above with regard to spelling, grammar, and punctuation?
    A. 1, 2, and 3 are correct, but 4 and 5 have errors.
    B. 2, 3, and 5 are correct, but 1 and 4 have errors.
    C. 3, 4, and 5 are correct, but 1 and 2 have errors.
    D. 1, 2, 3, and 5 are correct, but 4 has errors.

21._____

22. The one of the following sentences which is grammatically PREFERABLE to the others is:
    A. Our engineers will go over your blueprints so that you may have no problems in construction.
    B. For a long time he had been arguing that we, not he, are to blame for the confusion.
    C. I worked on his automobile for two hours and still cannot find out what is wrong with it.
    D. Accustomed to all kinds of hardships, fatigue seldom bothers veteran policemen.

22._____

23. The MOST accurate of the following sentences is:
    A. The commissioner, as well as his deputy and various bureau heads, were present.
    B. A new organization of employers and employees have been formed.
    C. One or the other of these men have been selected.
    D. The number of pages in the book is enough to discourage a reader.

23._____

24. The MOST accurate of the following sentences is: 24._____
    A. Between you and me, I think he is the better man.
    B. He was believed to be me.
    C. Is it us that you wish to see?
    D. The winners are him and her.

KEY (CORRECT ANSWERS)

1. C
2. A
3. C
4. A
5. B

6. C
7. D
8. C
9. B
10. A

11. B
12. B
13. D
14. B
15. D

16. A
17. C
18. A
19. D
20. B

21. B
22. A
23. D
24. A

REPORT WRITING
EXAMINATION SECTION
TEST 1

DIRECTIONS: Each question or incomplete statement is followed by several suggested answers or completions. Select the one that BEST answers the question or completes the statement. *PRINT THE LETTER OF THE CORRECT ANSWER IN THE SPACE AT THE RIGHT.*

1. Following are six steps that should be taken in the course of report preparation:
   I. Outlining the material for presentation in the report
   II. Analyzing and interpreting the facts
   III. Analyzing the problem
   IV. Reaching conclusions
   V. Writing, revising, and rewriting the final copy
   VI. Collecting data

   According to the principles of good report writing, the CORRECT order in which these steps should be taken is:
   A. VI, III, II, I, IV, V
   B. III, VI, II, IV, I, V
   C. III, VI, II, I, IV, V
   D. VI, II, III, IV, I, V

   1.____

2. Following are three statements concerning written reports:
   I. Clarity is generally more essential in oral reports than in written reports.
   II. Short sentences composed of simple words are generally preferred to complex sentences and difficult words.
   III. Abbreviations may be used whenever they are customary and will not distract the attention of the reader.

   Which of the following choices correctly classifies the above statements in to those which are valid and those which are not valid?
   A. I and II are valid, but III is not valid
   B. I is valid, but II and III are not valid.
   C. II and III are valid, but I is not valid.
   D. III is valid, but I and II are not valid.

   2.____

3. In order to produce a report written in a style that is both understandable and effective, an investigator should apply the principles of unit, coherence, and emphasis.
   The one of the following which is the BEST example of the principle of coherence is
   A. interlinking sentences so that thoughts flow smoothly
   B. having each sentence express a single idea to facilitate comprehension
   C. arranging important points in prominent positions so they are not overlooked
   D. developing the main idea fully to insure complete consideration

   3.____

4. Assume that a supervisor is preparing a report recommending that a standard work procedure be changed.
Of the following, the MOST important information that he should include in this report is
   A. a complete description of the present procedure
   B. the details and advantages of the recommended procedure
   C. the type and amount of retraining needed
   D. the percentage of men who favor the change

5. When you include in your report on an inspection some information which you have obtained from other individuals, it is MOST important that
   A. this information have no bearing on the work these other people are performing
   B. you do not report as fact the opinions of other individuals
   C. you keep the source of the information confidential
   D. you do not tell the other individuals that their statements will be included in your report

6. Before turning in a report of an investigator of an accident, you discover some additional information you did not know about when you wrote the report. Whether or not you re-write your report to include this additional information should depend MAINLY on the
   A. source of this additional information
   B. established policy covering the subject matter of the report
   C. length of the report and the time it would take you to re-write it
   D. bearing this additional information will have on the conclusions in the report

7. The MOST desirable *first* step in the planning of a written report is to
   A. ascertain what necessary information is readily available in the files
   B. outline the methods you will employ to get the necessary information
   C. determine the objectives and uses of the report
   D. estimate the time and cost required to complete the report

8. In writing a report, the practice of taking up the least important points and the most important points last is a
   A. *good* technique since the final points made in a report will make the greatest impression on the reader
   B. *good* technique since the material is presented in a more logical manner and will lead directly to the conclusions
   C. *poor* technique since the reader's time is wasted by having to review irrelevant information before finishing the report
   D. *poor* technique since it may cause the reader to lose interest in the report and arrive at incorrect conclusions about the report

9. Which one of the following serves as the BEST guideline for you to follow for effective written reports?
   Keep sentences
   A. short and limit sentences to one thought
   B. short and use as many thoughts as possible
   C. long and limit sentences to one thought
   D. long and use as many thoughts as possible

9.____

10. One method by which a supervisor might prepare written reports to management is to begin with the conclusions, results, or summary, and to follow this with the supporting data.
    The BEST reason why management may *prefer* this form of report is that
    A. management lacks the specific training to understand the data
    B. the data completely supports the conclusions
    C. time is saved by getting to the conclusions of the report first
    D. the data contains all the information that is required for making the conclusions

10.____

11. When making written reports, it is MOST important that they be
    A. well-worded   B. accurate as to the facts
    C. brief   D. submitted immediately

11.____

12. Of the following, the MOST important reason for a supervisor to prepare good written reports is that
    A. a supervisor is rated on the quality of his reports
    B. decisions are often made on the basis of the reports
    C. such reports take less time for superiors to review
    D. such reports demonstrate efficiency of department operations

12.____

13. Of the following, the BEST test of a good report is whether it
    A. provides the information needed
    B. shows the good sense of the writer
    C. is prepared according to a proper format
    D. is grammatical and neat

13.____

14. When a supervisor writes a report, he can BEST show that he has a understanding of the subject of the report by
    A. including necessary facts and omitting nonessential details
    B. using statistical data
    C. giving his conclusions but not the data on which they are based
    D. using a technical vocabulary

14.____

15. Suppose you and another supervisor on the same level are assigned to work together on a report. You disagree strongly with one of the recommendations the other supervisor wants to include in the report but you cannot change his views.

15.____

Of the following, it would be BEST that
- A. you refuse to accept responsibility for the report
- B. you ask that someone else be assigned to this project to replace you
- C. each of you state his own ideas about this recommendation in the report
- D. you give in to the other supervisor's opinion for the sake of harmony

16. Standardized forms are often provided for submitting reports.
Of the following, the MOST important advantage of using standardized forms for reports is that
    - A. they take less time to prepare than individually written reports
    - B. the person making the report can omit information he considers unimportant
    - C. the responsibility for preparing these reports can be turned over to subordinates
    - D. necessary information is less likely to be omitted

16.____

17. A report which may BEST be classed as a *periodic* report is one which
    - A. requires the same type of information at regular intervals
    - B. contains detailed information which is to be retained in permanent records
    - C. is prepared whenever a special situation occurs
    - D. lists information in graphic form

17.____

18. In the writing of reports or letters, the ideas presented in a paragraph are usually of unequal importance and require varying degrees of emphasis.
All of the following are methods of placing extra stress on an idea EXCEPT
    - A. repeating it in a number of forms
    - B. placing it in the middle of the paragraph
    - C. placing it either at the beginning or at the end of a paragraph
    - D. underlining it

18.____

Questions 19-25.

DIRECTIONS: Questions 19 through 25 concern the subject of report writing and are based on the information and incidents described in the following paragraph. (In answering these questions, assume that the facts and incidents in the paragraph are true.)

On December 15, at 8 A.M., seven Laborers reported to Foreman Joseph Meehan in the Greenbranch Yard in Queens. Meehan instructed the men to load some 50-pound boxes of books on a truck for delivery to an agency building in Brooklyn. Meehan told the men that, because the boxes were rather heavy, two men should work together, helping each other lift and load each box. Since Michael Harper, one of the Laborers, was without a partner, Meehan helped him with the boxes for a while. When Meehan was called to the telephone in a nearby building, however, Harper decided to lift a box himself. He appeared able to lift the box, but, as he got the box halfway up, he cried out that he had a sharp pain in his back. Another Laborer, Jorge Ortiz, who was passing by, ran over to help Harper put the box down. Harper suddenly dropped the box, which fell on Ortiz' right foot. By this time, Meehan had come out of the building. He immediately helped get the box off Ortiz' foot and had both men lie down. Meehan covered the men with blankets and called an ambulance, which arrived a half hour later. At the hospital, the doctor said that the X-ray results showed that Ortiz' right foot was broken in three places.

19. What would be the BEST term to use in a report describing the injury of Jorge Ortiz?
    A. Strain B. Fracture C. Hernia D. Hemorrhage

    19.____

20. Which of the following would be the MOST accurate summary for the Foreman to put in his report of the incident?
    A. Ortiz attempted to help Harper carry a box which was too heavy for one person, but Harper dropped it before Ortiz got there.
    B. Ortiz tried to help Harper carry a box but Harper got a pain in his back and accidentally dropped the box on Ortiz' foot.
    C. Harper refused to follow Meehan's orders and lifted a box too heavy for him; he deliberately dropped it when Ortiz tried to help him carry it.
    D. Harper lifted a box and felt a pain in his back; Ortiz tried to help Harper put the box down but Harper accidentally dropped it on Ortiz' foot.

    20.____

21. One of the Laborers at the scene of the accident was asked his version of the incident.
    Which information obtained from this witness would be LEAST important for including in the accident report?
    A. His opinion as to the cause of the accident
    B. How much of the accident he saw
    C. His personal opinion of the victims
    D. His name and address

    21.____

22. What should be the MAIN objective of writing a report about the incident described in the above paragraph? To
    A. describe the important elements in the accident situation
    B. recommend that such Laborers as Ortiz be advised not to interfere in another's work unless given specific instructions
    C. analyze the problems occurring when there are not enough workers to perform a certain task
    D. illustrate the hazards involved in performing routine everyday tasks

    22.____

23. Which of the following is information *missing* from the above passage but which *should* be included in a report of the incident? The
    A. name of the Laborer's immediate supervisor
    B. contents of the boxes
    C. time at which the accident occurred
    D. object or action that caused the injury to Ortiz' foot

    23.____

24. According to the description of the incident, the accident occurred because
    A. Ortiz attempted to help Harper who resisted his help
    B. Harper failed to follow instructions given him by Meehan
    C. Meehan was not supervising his men as closely as he should have
    D. Harper was not strong enough to carry the box once he lifted it

    24.____

25. Which of the following is MOST important for a foreman to avoid when writing up an official accident report?   25.____
    A. Using technical language to describe equipment involved in the accident
    B. Putting in details which might later be judged unnecessary
    C. Giving an opinion as to conditions that contributed to the accident
    D. Recommending discipline for employees who, in his opinion, caused the accident

KEY (CORRECT ANSWERS)

1.	B	11.	B
2.	C	12.	B
3.	A	13.	A
4.	B	14.	A
5.	B	15.	C
6.	D	16.	D
7.	C	17.	A
8.	D	18.	B
9.	A	19.	B
10.	C	20.	D

21.	C
22.	A
23.	C
24.	B
25.	D

TEST 2

DIRECTIONS: Each question or incomplete statement is followed by several suggested answers or completions. Select the one that BEST answers the question or completes the statement. *PRINT THE LETTER OF THE CORRECT ANSWER IN THE SPACE AT THE RIGHT.*

1. Lieutenant X is preparing a report to submit to his commanding officer in order to get approval of a plan of operation he has developed.
   The report starts off with the statement of the problem and continues with the details of the problem. It contains factual information gathered with the help of field and operational personnel. It contains a final conclusion and recommendation for action. The recommendation is supplemented by comments from other precinct staff members on how the recommendations will affect their areas of responsibility. The report also includes directives and general orders ready for the commanding officer's signature. In addition, it has two statements of objections presented by two precinct staff members.
   Which one of the following, if any, is either an item that Lieutenant X should have included in his report and which is not mentioned above, or is an item which Lieutenant X improperly did include in his report?
   A. Considerations of alternative courses of action and their consequences should have been covered in the report.
   B. The additions containing undocumented objections to the recommended course of action should not have been included as part of the report.
   C. A statement on the qualifications of Lieutenant X, which would support his expertness in the field under consideration, should have been included in the report.
   D. The directives and general orders should not have been prepared and included in the report until the commanding officer had approved the recommendations.
   E. None of the above, since Lieutenant X's report was both proper and complete.

   1.____

2. During a visit to a section, the district supervisor criticizes the method being used by the assistant foreman to prepare a certain report and orders him to modify the method. This change ordered by the district supervisor is in direct conflict with the specific orders of the foreman.
   In this situation, it would be BEST for the assistant foreman to
   A. change the method and tell the foreman about the change at the first opportunity
   B. change the method and rely on the district supervisor to notify the foreman
   C. report the matter to the foreman and delay the preparation of the report
   D. ask the district supervisor to discuss the matter with the foreman but use the old method for the time being

   2.____

3. A department officer should realize that the MOST usual reason for writing a report is to
   A. give orders and follow up their execution
   B. establish a permanent record
   C. raise questions
   D. supply information

4. A very important report which is being prepared by a department officer will soon be due on the desk of the district supervisor. No typing help is available at this time for the officer.
   For the officer to write out this report in longhand in such a situation would be
   A. *bad*; such a report would not make the impression a typed report would
   B. *good*; it is important to get the report in on time
   C. *bad*; the district supervisor should not be required to read longhand reports
   D. *good*; it would call attention to the difficult conditions under which this section must work

5. In a well-written report, the length of each paragraph in the report should be
   A. varied according to the content
   B. not over 300 words
   C. pretty nearly the same
   D. gradually longer as the report is developed and written

6. A clerk in the headquarters office complains to you about the way in which you are filing out a certain report.
   It would be BEST for you to
   A. tell the clerk that you are following official procedures in filling out the report
   B. ask to be referred to the clerk's superior
   C. ask the clerk exactly what is wrong with the way in which you are filling out the report
   D. tell the clerk that you are following the directions of the district supervisor

7. The use of an outline to help in writing a report is
   A. *desirable*, in order to insure good organization and coverage
   B. *necessary*, so it can be used as an introduction to the report itself
   C. *undesirable*, since it acts as a straightjacket and may result in an unbalanced report
   D. *desirable*, if you know your immediate supervisor reads reports with extreme care and attention

8. It is advisable that a department officer do his paper work and report writing as soon as he has completed an inspection MAINLY because
   A. there are usually deadlines to be met
   B. it insures a steady work-flow
   C. he may not have time for this later
   D. the facts are then freshest in his mind

9. Before you turn in a report you have written of an investigation that you have made, you discover some additional information you didn't know about before. Whether or not you re-write the report to include this additional information should depend MAINLY on the
   A. amount of time remaining before the report is due
   B. established policy of the department covering the subject matter of the report
   C. bearing this information will have on the conclusions of the report
   D. number of people who will eventually review the report

9.____

10. When a supervisory officer submits a periodic report to the district supervisor, he should realize that the CHIEF importance of such a report is that it
    A. is the principal method of checking on the efficiency of the supervisor and his subordinates
    B. is something to which frequent reference will be made
    C. eliminates the need for any personal follow-up or inspection by higher echelons
    D. permits the district supervisor to exercise his functions of direction, supervision, and control better

10.____

11. Conclusions and recommendations are usually placed at the end rather than at the beginning of a report because
    A. the person preparing the report may decide to change some of the conclusions and recommendations before he reaches the end of the report
    B. they are the most important part of the report
    C. they can be judged better by the person to whom the report is sent after he reads the facts and investigators which come earlier in the report
    D. they can be referred to quickly when needed without reading the rest of the report

11.____

12. The use of the same method of record-keeping and reporting by all agency sections is
    A. *desirable*, MAINLY because it saves time in section operations
    B. *undesirable*, MAINLY because it kills the initiative of the individual section foreman
    C. *desirable*, MAINLY because it will be easier for the administrator to evaluate and compare section operations
    D. *undesirable*, MAINLY because operations vary from section to section and uniform record-keeping and reporting is not appropriate

12.____

13. The GREATEST benefit the section officer will have from keeping complete and accurate records and reports of section operations is that
    A. he will find it easier to run his section efficiently
    B. he will need less equipment
    C. he will need less manpower
    D. the section will run smoothly when he is out

13.____

14. You have prepared a report to your superior and are ready to send it forward. But on re-reading it, you think some parts are not clearly expressed and your superior ay have difficulty getting your point.
    Of the following, it would be BEST for you to
    A. give the report to one of your men to read, and if he has no trouble understanding it send it through
    B. forward the report and call your superior the next day to ask whether it was all right
    C. forward the report as is; higher echelons should be able to understand any report prepared by a section officer
    D. do the report over, re-writing the sections you are in doubt about

14._____

15. The BEST of the following statements concerning reports is that
    A. a carelessly written report may give the reader an impression of inaccuracy
    B. correct grammar and English are unimportant if the main facts are given
    C. every man should be required to submit a daily work report
    D. the longer and more wordy a report is, the better it will read

15._____

16. In writing a report, the question of whether or not to include certain material could be determined BEST by considering the
    A. amount of space the material will occupy in the report
    B. amount of time to be spent in gathering the material
    C. date of the material
    D. value of the material to the superior who will read the report

16._____

17. Suppose you are submitting a fairly long report to your superior.
    The one of the following sections that should come FIRST in this report is a
    A. description of how you gathered material
    B. discussion of possible objections to your recommendations
    C. plan of how your recommendations can be put into practice
    D. statement of the problem dealt with

17._____

Questions 18-20.

DIRECTIONS: A foreman is asked to write a report on the incident described in the following passage. Answer Questions 18 through 20 based on the following information.

On March 10, Henry Moore, a laborer, was in the process of transferring some equipment from the machine shop to the third floor. He was using a dolly to perform this task and, as he was wheeling the material through the machine shop, laborer Bob Greene called to him. As Henry turned to respond to Bob, he jammed the dolly into Larry Mantell's leg, knocking Larry down in the process and causing the heavy drill that Larry was holding to fall on Larry's foot. Larry started rubbing his foot and then, infuriated, jumped up and punched Henry in the jaw. The force of the blow drove Henry's head back against the wall. Henry did not fight back; he appeared to be dazed. An ambulance was called to take Henry to the hospital, and the ambulance attendant told the foreman that it appeared likely that Henry had suffered a concussion. Larry's injuries consisted of some bruises, but he refused medical attention.

18. An adequate report of the above incident should give as minimum information
the names of the persons involved, the names of the witnesses, the date and
the time that each event took place, and the
    A. names of the ambulance attendants
    B. names of all the employees working in the machine shop
    C. location where the accident occurred
    D. nature of the previous safety training each employee had been given

18.____

19. The only one of the following which is NOT a fact is
    A. Bob called to Henry
    B. Larry suffered a concussion
    C. Larry rubbed his foot
    D. the incident took place in the machine shop

19.____

20. Which of the following would be the MOST accurate summary of the incident
for the foreman to put in his report of the accident?
    A. Larry Mantell punched Henry Moore because a drill fell on his foot and he
       was angry. Then Henry fell and suffered a concussion.
    B. Henry Moore accidentally jammed a dolly into Larry Mantell's foot,
       knocking Larry down. Larry punched Henry, pushing him into the wall
       and causing him to bang his head against the wall.
    C. Bob Greene called Henry Moore. A dolly than jammed into Larry Mantell
       and knocked him down. Larry punched Henry who tripped and suffered
       some bruises. An ambulance was called.
    D. A drill fell on Larry Mantell's foot. Larry jumped up suddenly and punched
       Henry Moore and pushed him into the wall. Henry may have suffered a
       concussion as a result of falling.

20.____

Questions 21-25.

DIRECTIONS: Questions 21 through 25 are to be answered ONLY on the basis of the
information provided in the following passage.

A written report is a communication of information from one person to another. It is an
account of some matter especially investigated, however routine that matter may be. The
ultimate basis of any good written report is facts, which become known through observation and
verification. Good written reports may seem to be no more than general ideas and opinions.
However, in such cases, the facts leading to these opinions were gathered, verified, and
reported earlier, and the opinions are dependent upon these facts. Good style, proper form,
and emphasis cannot make a good written report out of unreliable information and bad
judgment; but, on the other hand, solid investigation and brilliant thinking are not likely to
become very useful until they are effectively communicated to others. If a person's work calls
for written reports, then his work is often no better than his written reports.

21. Based on the information in the above passage, it can be concluded that opinions expressed in a report should be
    A. based on facts which are gathered and reported
    B. emphasized repeatedly when they result from a special investigation
    C. kept to a minimum
    D. separated from the body of the report

    21.____

22. In the above passage, the one of the following which is mentioned as a way of establishing facts is
    A. authority
    B. communication
    C. reporting
    D. verification

    22.____

23. According to the above passage, the characteristic shared by ALL written reports is that they are
    A. accounts of routine matters
    B. transmissions of information
    C. reliable and logical
    D. written in proper form

    23.____

24. Which of the following conclusions can logically be drawn from the information given in the above passage?
    A. Brilliant thinking can make up for unreliable information in a report.
    B. One method of judging an individual's work is the quality of the written reports he is required to submit.
    C. Proper form and emphasis can make a good report out of unreliable information.
    D. Good written reports that seem to be no more than general ideas should be rewritten.

    24.____

25. Which of the following suggested titles would be MOST appropriate for this passage?
    A. Gathering and Organizing Facts
    B. Techniques of Observation
    C. Nature and Purpose of Reports
    D. Reports and Opinions: Differences and Similarities

    25.____

KEY (CORRECT ANSWERS)

1.	A	11.	C
2.	A	12.	C
3.	D	13.	A
4.	B	14.	D
5.	A	15.	A
6.	C	16.	D
7.	A	17.	D
8.	D	18.	C
9.	C	19.	B
10.	D	20.	B

21. A
22. D
23. B
24. B
25. C

TEST 3

DIRECTIONS: Each question or incomplete statement is followed by several suggested answers or completions. Select the one that BEST answers the question or completes the statement. *PRINT THE LETTER OF THE CORRECT ANSWER IN THE SPACE AT THE RIGHT.*

Questions 1-5.

DIRECTIONS: The following is an accident report similar to those used in departments for reporting accidents. Questions 1 through 5 are be answered using ONLY the information given in this report.

ACCIDENT REPORT

FROM: John Doe	DATE OF REPORT: June 23	
TITLE: Sanitation Worker		
DATE OF ACCIDENT: June 22 time 3 ~~AM~~ PM	CITY: Metropolitan	
PLACE: 1489 Third Avenue		
VEHICLE NO. 1	VEHICLE NO. 2	
OPERATOR: John Doe, Sanitation Worker Title	OPERATOR: Richard Roe	
VEHICLE CODE NO: 14-238	ADDRESS: 498 High Street	
LICENSE NO.: 0123456	OWNER: Henry Roe ADDRESS: 786 E.83 St.	LIC. NO.: 5N1492
DESCRIPTION OF ACCIDENT: Light green Chevrolet sedan while trying to pass drove in to rear side of sanitation truck which had stopped to collect garbage. No one was injured but there was property damage.		
NATURE OF DAMAGE TO PRIVATE VEHICLE: Right front fender crushed, bumper bent		
DAMAGE TO CITY VEHICLE: Front of left rear fender pushed in. Paint scraped.		
NAME OF WITNESS: Frank Brown	ADDRESS: 48 Kingsway	
SIGNATURE OF PERSON MAKING THIS REPORT *John Doe*	BADGE NO.: 428	

1. Of the following, the one which has been omitted from this accident report is the   1.____
    A. location of the accident
    B. drivers of the vehicles involved
    C. traffic situation at the time of the accident
    D. owners of the vehicles involved

2. The address of the driver of Vehicle No. 1 is not required because he   2.____
    A. is employed by the department   B. is not the owner of the vehicle
    C. reported the accident   D. was injured in the accident

3. The report indicates that the driver of Vehicle No. 2 was PROBABLY   3.____
    A. passing on the wrong side of the truck
    B. not wearing his glasses
    C. not injured in the accident
    D driving while intoxicated

4. The number of people *specifically* referred to in this report is 4.____
   A. 3   B. 4   C. 5   D. 6

5. The license number of Vehicle No. 1 is 5.____
   A. 428   B. 5N1492   C. 14-238   D. 0123456

6. In a report of unlawful entry into department premises, it is LEAST important to include the 6.____
   A. estimated value of the property missing
   B. general description of the premises
   C. means used to get into the premises
   D. time and date of entry

7. In a report of an accident, it is LEAST important to include the 7.____
   A. name of the insurance company of the person injured in the accident
   B. probable cause of the accident
   C. time and place of the accident
   D. names and addresses of all witnesses of the accident

8. Of the following, the one which is NOT required in the preparation of a weekly functional expense report is the 8.____
   A. hourly distribution of the time by proper heading in accordance with the actual work performed
   B. signatures of officers not involved in the preparation of the report
   C. time records of the men who appear on the payroll of the respective locations
   D. time records of men working in other districts assigned to this location

KEY (CORRECT ANSWERS)

1.	C	5.	D
2.	A	6.	B
3.	C	7.	A
4.	B	8.	B

PHILOSOPHY, PRINCIPLES, PRACTICES, AND TECHNICS
OF
SUPERVISION, ADMINISTRATION, MANAGEMENT, AND ORGANIZATION

TABLE OF CONTENTS

	Page
MEANING OF SUPERVISION	1
THE OLD AND THE NEW SUPERVISION	1
THE EIGHT (8) BASIC PRINCIPLES OF THE NEW SUPERVISION	1
I. Principle of Responsibility	1
II. Principle of Authority	2
III. Principle of Self-Growth	2
IV. Principle of Individual Worth	2
V. Principle of Creative Leadership	2
VI. Principle of Success and Failure	2
VII. Principle of Science	3
VIII. Principle of Cooperation	3
WHAT IS ADMINISTRATION?	3
I. Practices Commonly Classed as "Supervisory"	3
II. Practices Commonly Classed as "Administrative"	3
III. Practices Commonly Classed as Both "Supervisory" and "Administrative"	4
RESPONSIBILITIES OF THE SUPERVISOR	4
COMPETENCIES OF THE SUPERVISOR	4
THE PROFESSIONAL SUPERVISOR-EMPLOYEE RELATIONSHIP	4
MINI-TEXT IN SUPERVISION, ADMINISTRATION, MANAGEMENT, AND ORGANIZATION	5
I. Brief Highlights	5
A. Levels of Management	6
B. What the Supervisor Must Learn	6
C. A Definition of Supervision	6
D. Elements of the Team Concept	6
E. Principles of Organization	6
F. The Four Important Parts of Every Job	7
G. Principles of Delegation	7
H. Principles of Effective Communications	7
I. Principles of Work Improvement	7
J. Areas of Job Improvement	7
K. Seven Key Points in Making Improvements	8

	L.	Corrective Techniques for Job Improvement	8
	M.	A Planning Checklist	8
	N.	Five Characteristics of Good Directions	9
	O.	Types of Directions	9
	P.	Controls	9
	Q.	Orienting the New Employee	9
	R.	Checklist for Orienting New Employees	9
	S.	Principles of Learning	10
	T.	Causes of Poor Performance	10
	U.	Four Major Steps in On-the-Job Instructions	10
	V.	Employees Want Five Things	10
	W.	Some Don'ts in Regard to Praise	11
	X.	How to Gain Your Workers' Confidence	11
	Y.	Sources of Employee Problems	11
	Z.	The Supervisor's Key to Discipline	11
	AA.	Five Important Processes of Management	12
	BB.	When the Supervisor Fails to Plan	12
	CC.	Fourteen General Principles of Management	12
	DD.	Change	12
II.	Brief Topical Summaries		13
	A.	Who/What is the Supervisor?	13
	B.	The Sociology of Work	13
	C.	Principles and Practices of Supervision	14
	D.	Dynamic Leadership	14
	E.	Processes for Solving Problems	15
	F.	Training for Results	15
	G.	Health, Safety, and Accident Prevention	16
	H.	Equal Employment Opportunity	16
	I.	Improving Communications	16
	J.	Self-Development	17
	K.	Teaching and Training	17
		1. The Teaching Process	17
		a. Preparation	17
		b. Presentation	18
		c. Summary	18
		d. Application	18
		e. Evaluation	18
		2. Teaching Methods	18
		a. Lecture	18
		b. Discussion	18
		c. Demonstration	19
		d. Performance	19
		e. Which Method to Use	19

PHILOSOPHY, PRINCIPLES, PRACTICES, AND TECHNICS OF SUPERVISION, ADMINISTRATION, MANAGEMENT, AND ORGANIZATION

MEANING OF SUPERVISION

The extension of the democratic philosophy has been accompanied by an extension in the scope of supervision. Modern leaders and supervisors no longer think of supervision in the narrow sense of being confined chiefly to visiting employees, supplying materials, or rating the staff. They regard supervision as being intimately related to all the concerned agencies of society, they speak of the supervisor's function in terms of "growth," rather than the "improvement" of employees.

This modern concept of supervision may be defined as follows: Supervision is leadership and the development of leadership within groups which are cooperatively engaged in inspection, research, training, guidance, and evaluation.

THE OLD AND THE NEW SUPERVISION

TRADITIONAL
1. Inspection
2. Focused on the employee
3. Visitation
4. Random and haphazard
5. Imposed and authoritarian
6. One person usually

MODERN
1. Study and analysis
2. Focused on aims, materials, methods, supervisors, employees, environment
3. Demonstrations, intervisitation, workshops, directed reading, bulletins, etc.
4. Definitely organized and planned (scientific)
5. Cooperative and democratic
6. Many persons involved (creative)

THE EIGHT (8) BASIC PRINCIPLES OF THE NEW SUPERVISION

I. Principle of Responsibility
   Authority to act and responsibility for acting must be joined.
   A. If you give responsibility, give authority.
   B. Define employee duties clearly.
   C. Protect employees from criticism by others.
   D. Recognize the rights as well as obligations of employees.
   E. Achieve the aims of a democratic society insofar as it is possible within the area of your work.
   F. Establish a situation favorable to training and learning.
   G. Accept ultimate responsibility for everything done in your section, unit, office, division, department.
   H. Good administration and good supervision are inseparable.

II. Principle of Authority
   The success of the supervisor is measured by the extent to which the power of authority is not used.
   A. Exercise simplicity and informality in supervision
   B. Use the simplest machinery of supervision
   C. If it is good for the organization as a whole, it is probably justified.
   D. Seldom be arbitrary or authoritative.
   E. Do not base your work on the power of position or of personality.
   F. Permit and encourage the free expression of opinions.

III. Principle of Self-Growth
   The success of the supervisor is measured by the extent to which, and the speed with which, he is no longer needed.
   A. Base criticism on principles, not on specifics.
   B. Point out higher activities to employees.
   C. Train for self-thinking by employees to meet new situations.
   D. Stimulate initiative, self-reliance, and individual responsibility
   E. Concentrate on stimulating the growth of employees rather than on removing defects.

IV. Principle of Individual Worth
   Respect for the individual is a paramount consideration in supervision.
   A. Be human and sympathetic in dealing with employees.
   B. Don't nag about things to be done.
   C. Recognize the individual differences among employees and seek opportunities to permit best expression of each personality.

V. Principle of Creative Leadership
   The best supervision is that which is not apparent to the employee.
   A. Stimulate, don't drive employees to creative action.
   B. Emphasize doing good things.
   C. Encourage employees to do what they do best.
   D. Do not be too greatly concerned with details of subject or method.
   E. Do not be concerned exclusively with immediate problems and activities.
   F. Reveal higher activities and make them both desired and maximally possible.
   G. Determine procedures in the light of each situation but see that these are derived from a sound basic philosophy.
   H. Aid, inspire, and lead so as to liberate the creative spirit latent in all good employees.

VI. Principle of Success and Failure
   There are no unsuccessful employees, only unsuccessful supervisors who have failed to give proper leadership.
   A. Adapt suggestions to the capacities, attitudes, and prejudices of employees.
   B. Be gradual, be progressive, be persistent.
   C. Help the employee find the general principle; have the employee apply his own problem to the general principle.
   D. Give adequate appreciation for good work and honest effort.
   E. Anticipate employee difficulties and help to prevent them.
   F. Encourage employees to do the desirable things they will do anyway.
   G. Judge your supervision by the results it secures.

VII. Principle of Science
Successful supervision is scientific, objective, and experimental. It is based on facts, not on prejudices.
   A. Be cumulative in results.
   B. Never divorce your suggestions from the goals of training.
   C. Don't be impatient of results.
   D. Keep all matters on a professional, not a personal, level.
   E. Do not be concerned exclusively with immediate problems and activities.
   F. Use objective means of determining achievement and rating where possible.

VIII. Principle of Cooperation
Supervision is a cooperative enterprise between supervisor and employee.
   A. Begin with conditions as they are.
   B. Ask opinions of all involved when formulating policies.
   C. Organization is as good as its weakest link.
   D. Let employees help to determine policies and department programs.
   E. Be approachable and accessible—physically and mentally.
   F. Develop pleasant social relationships.

WHAT IS ADMINISTRATION

Administration is concerned with providing the environment, the material facilities, and the operational procedures that will promote the maximum growth and development of supervisors and employees. (Organization is an aspect and a concomitant of administration.)

There is no sharp line of demarcation between supervision and administration; these functions are intimately interrelated and, often, overlapping. They are complementary activities.

I. Practices Commonly Classed as "Supervisory"
   A. Conducting employees' conferences
   B. Visiting sections, units, offices, divisions, departments
   C. Arranging for demonstrations
   D. Examining plans
   E. Suggesting professional reading
   F. Interpreting bulletins
   G. Recommending in-service training courses
   H. Encouraging experimentation
   I. Appraising employee morale
   J. Providing for intervisitation

II. Practices Commonly Classified as "Administrative"
   A. Management of the office
   B. Arrangement of schedules for extra duties
   C. Assignment of rooms or areas
   D. Distribution of supplies
   E. Keeping records and reports
   F. Care of audio-visual materials
   G. Keeping inventory records
   H. Checking record cards and books

4

    I.   Programming special activities
    J.   Checking on the attendance and punctuality of employees

III.   Practices Commonly Classified as Both "Supervisory" and "Administrative"
    A.   Program construction
    B.   Testing or evaluating outcomes
    C.   Personnel accounting
    D.   Ordering instructional materials

RESPONSIBILITIES OF THE SUPERVISOR

A person employed in a supervisory capacity must constantly be able to improve his own efficiency and ability. He represent the employer to the employees and only continuous self-examination can make him a capable supervisor.

Leadership and training are the supervisor's responsibility. An efficient working unit is one in which the employees work with the supervisor. It is his job to bring out the best in his employees. He must always be relaxed, courteous, and calm in his association with his employees. Their feelings are important, and a harsh attitude does not develop the most efficient employees.

COMPETENCES OF THE SUPERVISOR

    I.   Complete knowledge of the duties and responsibilities of his position.
    II.   To be able to organize a job, plan ahead, and carry through.
    III.   To have self-confidence and initiative.
    IV.   To be able to handle the unexpected situation and make quick decisions.
    V.   To be able to properly train subordinates in the positions they are best suited for.
    VI.   To be able to keep good human relations among his subordinates.
    VII.   To be able to keep good human relations between his subordinates and himself and to earn their respect and trust.

THE PROFESSIONAL SUPERVISOR-EMPLOYEE RELATIONSHIP

There are two kinds of efficiency: one kind is only apparent and is produced in organizations through the exercise of mere discipline; this is but a simulation of the second, or true, efficiency which springs from spontaneous cooperation. If you are a manager, no matter how great or small your responsibility, it is your job, in the final analysis, to create and develop this involuntary cooperation among the people whom you supervise. For, no matter how powerful a combination of money, machines, and materials a company may have, this is a dead and sterile thing without a team of willing, thinking, and articulate people to guide it.

The following 21 points are presented as indicative of the exemplary basic relationship that should exist between supervisor and employee:

1. Each person wants to be liked and respected by his fellow employee and wants to be treated with consideration and respect by his superior.
2. The most competent employee will make an error. However, in a unit where good relations exist between the supervisor and his employees, tenseness and fear do not exist. Thus, errors are not hidden or covered up, and the efficiency of a unit is not impaired.

3. Subordinates resent rules, regulations, or orders that are unreasonable or unexplained.
4. Subordinates are quick to resent unfairness, harshness, injustices, and favoritism.
5. An employee will accept responsibility if he knows that he will be complimented for a job well done, and not too harshly chastised for failure; that his supervisor will check the cause of the failure, and, if it was the supervisor's fault, he will assume the blame therefore. If it was the employee's fault, his supervisor will explain the correct method or means of handling the responsibility.
6. An employee wants to receive credit for a suggestion he has made, that is used. If a suggestion cannot be used, the employee is entitled to an explanation. The supervisor should not say "no" and close the subject.
7. Fear and worry slow up a worker's ability. Poor working environment can impair his physical and mental health. A good supervisor avoids forceful methods, threats, and arguments to get a job done.
8. A forceful supervisor is able to train his employees individually and as a team, and is able to motivate them in the proper channels.
9. A mature supervisor is able to properly evaluate his subordinates and to keep them happy and satisfied.
10. A sensitive supervisor will never patronize his subordinates.
11. A worthy supervisor will respect his employees' confidences.
12. Definite and clear-cut responsibilities should be assigned to each executive.
13. Responsibility should always be coupled with corresponding authority.
14. No change should be made in the scope or responsibilities of a position without a definite understanding to that effect on the part of all persons concerned.
15. No executive or employee, occupying a single position in the organization, should be subject to definite orders from more than one source.
16. Orders should never be given to subordinates over the head of a responsible executive. Rather than do this, the officer in question should be supplanted.
17. Criticisms of subordinates should, whoever possible, be made privately, and in no case should a subordinate be criticized in the presence of executives or employees of equal or lower rank.
18. No dispute or difference between executives or employees as to authority or responsibilities should be considered too trivial for prompt and careful adjudication.
19. Promotions, wage changes, and disciplinary action should always be approved by the executive immediately superior to the one directly responsible.
20. No executive or employee should ever be required, or expected, to be at the same time an assistant to, and critic of, another.
21. Any executive whose work is subject to regular inspection should, wherever practicable, be given the assistance and facilities necessary to enable him to maintain an independent check of the quality of his work.

MINI-TEXT IN SUPERVISION, ADMINISTRATION, MANAGEMENT, AND ORGANIZATION

I. Brief Highlights

Listed concisely and sequentially are major headings and important data in the field for quick recall and review.

A. Levels of Management
Any organization of some size has several levels of management. In terms of a ladder, the levels are:

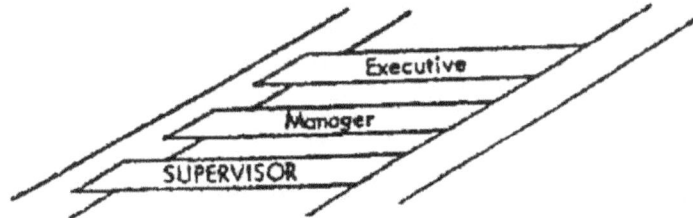

The first level is very important because it is the beginning point of management leadership.

B. What the Supervisor Must Learn
A supervisor must learn to:
1. Deal with people and their differences
2. Get the job done through people
3. Recognize the problems when they exist
4. Overcome obstacles to good performance
5. Evaluate the performance of people
6. Check his own performance in terms of accomplishment

C. A Definition of Supervisor
The term supervisor means any individual having authority, in the interests of the employer, to hire, transfer, suspend, lay-off, recall, promote, discharge, assign, reward, or discipline other employees or responsibility to direct them, or to adjust their grievances, or effectively to recommend such action, if, in connection with the foregoing, exercise of such authority is not of a merely routine or clerical nature but requires the use of independent judgment.

D. Elements of the Team Concept
What is involved in teamwork? The component parts are:
1. Members
2. A leader
3. Goals
4. Plans
5. Cooperation
6. Spirit

E. Principles of Organization
1. A team member must know what his job is.
2. Be sure that the nature and scope of a job are understood.
3. Authority and responsibility should be carefully spelled out.
4. A supervisor should be permitted to make the maximum number of decisions affecting his employees.
5. Employees should report to only one supervisor.
6. A supervisor should direct only as many employees as he can handle effectively.
7. An organization plan should be flexible.

8. Inspection and performance of work should be separate.
9. Organizational problems should receive immediate attention.
10. Assign work in line with ability and experience.

F. The Four Important Parts of Every Job
1. Inherent in every job is the *accountability* for results.
2. A second set of factors in every job is *responsibilities*.
3. Along with duties and responsibilities one must have the *authority* to act within certain limits without obtaining permission to proceed.
4. No job exists in a vacuum. The supervisor is surrounded by key *relationships*.

G. Principles of Delegation
Where work is delegated for the first time, the supervisor should think in terms of these questions:
1. Who is best qualified to do this?
2. Can an employee improve his abilities by doing this?
3. How long should an employee spend on this?
4. Are there any special problems for which he will need guidance?
5. How broad a delegation can I make?

H. Principles of Effective Communications
1. Determine the media.
2. To whom directed?
3. Identification and source authority.
4. Is communication understood?

I. Principles of Work Improvement
1. Most people usually do only the work which is assigned to them.
2. Workers are likely to fit assigned work into the time available to perform it.
3. A good workload usually stimulates output.
4. People usually do their best work when they know that results will be reviewed or inspected.
5. Employees usually feel that someone else is responsible for conditions of work, workplace layout, job methods, type of tools/equipment, and other such factors.
6. Employees are usually defensive about their job security.
7. Employees have natural resistance to change.
8. Employees can support or destroy a supervisor.
9. A supervisor usually earns the respect of his people through his personal example of diligence and efficiency.

J. Areas of Job Improvement
The areas of job improvement are quite numerous, but the most common ones which a supervisor can identify and utilize are:
1. Departmental layout
2. Flow of work
3. Workplace layout
4. Utilization of manpower
5. Work methods
6. Materials handling

7. Utilization
8. Motion economy

K. Seven Key Points in Making Improvements
1. Select the job to be improved
2. Study how it is being done now
3. Question the present method
4. Determine actions to be taken
5. Chart proposed method
6. Get approval and apply
7. Solicit worker participation

l. Corrective Techniques of Job Improvement
Specific Problems
1. Size of workload
2. Inability to meet schedules
3. Strain and fatigue
4. Improper use of men and skills
5. Waste, poor quality, unsafe conditions
6. Bottleneck conditions that hinder output
7. Poor utilization of equipment and machine
8. Efficiency and productivity of labor

General Improvement
1. Departmental layout
2. Flow of work
3. Work plan layout
4. Utilization of manpower
5. Work methods
6. Materials handling
7. Utilization of equipment
8. Motion economy

Corrective Techniques
1. Study with scale model
2. Flow chart study
3. Motion analysis
4. Comparison of units produced to standard allowance
5. Methods analysis
6. Flow chart and equipment study
7. Down time vs. running time
8. Motion analysis

M. A Planning Checklist
1. Objectives
2. Controls
3. Delegations
4. Communications
5. Resources
6. Manpower

7. Equipment
8. Supplies and materials
9. Utilization of time
10. Safety
11. Money
12. Work
13. Timing of improvements

N. Five Characteristics of Good Directions
In order to get results, directions must be:
1. Possible of accomplishment
2. Agreeable with worker interests
3. Related to mission
4. Planned and complete
5. Unmistakably clear

O. Types of Directions
1. Demands or direct orders
2. Requests
3. Suggestion or implication
4. volunteering

P. Controls
A typical listing of the overall areas in which the supervisor should establish controls might be:
1. Manpower
2. Materials
3. Quality of work
4. Quantity of work
5. Time
6. Space
7. Money
8. Methods

Q. Orienting the New Employee
1. Prepare for him
2. Welcome the new employee
3. Orientation for the job
4. Follow-up

R. Checklist for Orienting New Employees   Yes   No
1. Do you appreciate the feelings of new employees
   when they first report for work?   ___   ___
2. Are you aware of the fact that the new employee must
   make a big adjustment to his job?   ___   ___
3. Have you given him good reasons for liking the job and
   the organization?   ___   ___
4. Have you prepared for his first day on the job?   ___   ___
5. Did you welcome him cordially and make him feel needed?   ___   ___

	Yes	No

6. Did you establish rapport with him so that he feels free to talk and discuss matters with you? ___ ___
7. Did you explain his job to him and his relationship to you? ___ ___
8. Does he know that his work will be evaluated periodically on a basis that is fair and objective? ___ ___
9. Did you introduce him to his fellow workers in such a way that they are likely to accept him? ___ ___
10. Does he know what employee benefits he will receive? ___ ___
11. Does he understand the importance of being on the job and what to do if he must leave his duty station? ___ ___
12. Has he been impressed with the importance of accident prevention and safe practice? ___ ___
13. Does he generally know his way around the department? ___ ___
14. Is he under the guidance of a sponsor who will teach the right way of doing things? ___ ___
15. Do you plan to follow-up so that he will continue to adjust successfully to his job? ___ ___

S. Principles of Learning
   1. Motivation
   2. Demonstration or explanation
   3. Practice

T. Causes of Poor Performance
   1. Improper training for job
   2. Wrong tools
   3. Inadequate directions
   4. Lack of supervisory follow-up
   5. Poor communications
   6. Lack of standards of performance
   7. Wrong work habits
   8. Low morale
   9. Other

U. Four Major Steps in On-The-Job Instruction
   1. Prepare the worker
   2. Present the operation
   3. Tryout performance
   4. Follow-up

V. Employees Want Five Things
   1. Security
   2. Opportunity
   3. Recognition
   4. Inclusion
   5. Expression

11

W. Some Don'ts in Regard to Praise
1. Don't praise a person for something he hasn't done.
2. Don't praise a person unless you can be sincere.
3. Don't be sparing in praise just because your superior withholds it from you.
4. Don't let too much time elapse between good performance and recognition of it

X. How to Gain Your Workers' Confidence
Methods of developing confidence include such things as:
1. Knowing the interests, habits, hobbies of employees
2. Admitting your own inadequacies
3. Sharing and telling of confidence in others
4. Supporting people when they are in trouble
5. Delegating matters that can be well handled
6. Being frank and straightforward about problems and working conditions
7. Encouraging others to bring their problems to you
8. Taking action on problems which impede worker progress

Y. Sources of Employee Problems
On-the-job causes might be such things as:
1. A feeling that favoritism is exercised in assignments
2. Assignment of overtime
3. An undue amount of supervision
4. Changing methods or systems
5. Stealing of ideas or trade secrets
6. Lack of interest in job
7. Threat of reduction in force
8. Ignorance or lack of communications
9. Poor equipment
10. Lack of knowing how supervisor feels toward employee
11. Shift assignments

Off-the-job problems might have to do with:
1. Health
2. Finances
3. Housing
4. Family

Z. The Supervisor's Key to Discipline
There are several key points about discipline which the supervisor should keep in mind:
1. Job discipline is one of the disciplines of life and is directed by the supervisor.
2. It is more important to correct an employee fault than to fix blame for it.
3. Employee performance is affected by problems both on the job and off.
4. Sudden or abrupt changes in behavior can be indications of important employee problems.
5. Problems should be dealt with as soon as possible after they are identified.
6. The attitude of the supervisor may have more to do with solving problems than the techniques of problem solving.
7. Correction of employee behavior should be resorted to only after the supervisor is sure that training or counseling will not be helpful.

8. Be sure to document your disciplinary actions.
9. Make sure that you are disciplining on the basis of facts rather than personal feelings.
10. Take each disciplinary step in order, being careful not to make snap judgments, or decisions based on impatience.

AA. Five Important Processes of Management
1. Planning
2. Organizing
3. Scheduling
4. Controlling
5. Motivating

BB. When the Supervisor Fails to Plan
1. Supervisor creates impression of not knowing his job
2. May lead to excessive overtime
3. Job runs itself—supervisor lacks control
4. Deadlines and appointments missed
5. Parts of the work go undone
6. Work interrupted by emergencies
7. Sets a bad example
8. Uneven workload creates peaks and valleys
9. Too much time on minor details at expense of more important tasks

CC. Fourteen General Principles of Management
1. Division of work
2. Authority and responsibility
3. Discipline
4. Unity of command
5. Unity of direction
6. Subordination of individual interest to general interest
7. Remuneration of personnel
8. Centralization
9. Scalar chain
10. Order
11. Equity
12. Stability of tenure of personnel
13. Initiative
14. Esprit de corps

DD. Change

Bringing about change is perhaps attempted more often, and yet less well understood, than anything else the supervisor does. How do people generally react to change? (People tend to resist change that is imposed upon them by other individuals or circumstances.

Change is characteristic of every situation. It is a part of every real endeavor where the efforts of people are concerned.

1. Why do people resist change?
   People may resist change because of:
   a. Fear of the unknown
   b. Implied criticism
   c. Unpleasant experiences in the past
   d. Fear of loss of status
   e. Threat to the ego
   f. Fear of loss of economic stability

2. How can we best overcome the resistance to change?
   In initiating change, take these steps:
   a. Get ready to sell
   b. Identify sources of help
   c. Anticipate objections
   d. Sell benefits
   e. Listen in depth
   f. Follow up

II. Brief Topical Summaries

   A. Who/What is the Supervisor?
      1. The supervisor is often called the "highest level employee and the lowest level manager."
      2. A supervisor is a member of both management and the work group. He acts as a bridge between the two.
      3. Most problems in supervision are in the area of human relations, or people problems.
      4. Employees expect: Respect, opportunity to learn and to advance, and a sense of belonging, and so forth.
      5. Supervisors are responsible for directing people and organizing work. Planning is of paramount importance.
      6. A position description is a set of duties and responsibilities inherent to a given position.
      7. It is important to keep the position description up-to-date and to provide each employee with his own copy.

   B. The Sociology of Work
      1. People are alike in many ways; however, each individual is unique.
      2. The supervisor is challenged in getting to know employee differences. Acquiring skills in evaluating individuals is an asset.
      3. Maintaining meaningful working relationships in the organization is of great importance.
      4. The supervisor has an obligation to help individuals to develop to their fullest potential.
      5. Job rotation on a planned basis helps to build versatility and to maintain interest and enthusiasm in work groups.
      6. Cross training (job rotation) provides backup skills.

7. The supervisor can help reduce tension by maintaining a sense of humor, providing guidance to employees, and by making reasonable and timely decisions. Employees respond favorably to working under reasonably predictable circumstances.
8. Change is characteristic of all managerial behavior. The supervisor must adjust to changes in procedures, new methods, technological changes, and to a number of new and sometimes challenging situations.
9. To overcome the natural tendency for people to resist change, the supervisor should become more skillful in initiating change.

C. Principles and Practices of Supervision
1. Employees should be required to answer to only one superior.
2. A supervisor can effectively direct only a limited number of employees, depending upon the complexity, variety, and proximity of the jobs involved.
3. The organizational chart presents the organization in graphic form. It reflects lines of authority and responsibility as well as interrelationships of units within the organization.
4. Distribution of work can be improved through an analysis using the "Work Distribution Chart."
5. The "Work Distribution Chart" reflects the division of work within a unit in understandable form.
6. When related tasks are given to an employee, he has a better chance of increasing his skills through training.
7. The individual who is given the responsibility for tasks must also be given the appropriate authority to insure adequate results.
8. The supervisor should delegate repetitive, routine work. Preparation of recurring reports, maintaining leave and attendance records are some examples.
9. Good discipline is essential to good task performance. Discipline is reflected in the actions of employees on the job in the absence of supervision.
10. Disciplinary action may have to be taken when the positive aspects of discipline have failed. Reprimand, warning, and suspension are examples of disciplinary action.
11. If a situation calls for a reprimand, be sure it is deserved and remember it is to be done in private.

D. Dynamic Leadership
1. A style is a personal method or manner of exerting influence.
2. Authoritarian leaders often see themselves as the source of power and authority.
3. The democratic leader often perceives the group as the source of authority and power.
4. Supervisors tend to do better when using the pattern of leadership that is most natural for them.
5. Social scientists suggest that the effective supervisor use the leadership style that best fits the problem or circumstances involved.
6. All four styles—telling, selling, consulting, joining—have their place. Using one does not preclude using the other at another time.

7. The theory X point of view assumes that the average person dislikes work, will avoid it whenever possible, and must be coerced to achieve organizational objectives.
8. The theory Y point of view assumes that the average person considers work to be a natural as play, and, when the individual is committed, he requires little supervision or direction to accomplish desired objectives.
9. The leader's basic assumptions concerning human behavior and human nature affect his actions, decisions, and other managerial practices.
10. Dissatisfaction among employees is often present, but difficult to isolate. The supervisor should seek to weaken dissatisfaction by keeping promises, being sincere and considerate, keeping employees informed, and so forth.
11. Constructive suggestions should be encouraged during the natural progress of the work.

E. Processes for Solving Problems
1. People find their daily tasks more meaningful and satisfying when they can improve them.
2. The causes of problems, or the key factors, are often hidden in the background. Ability to solve problems often involves the ability to isolate them from their backgrounds. There is some substance to the cliché that some persons "can't see the forest for the trees."
3. New procedures are often developed from old ones. Problems should be broken down into manageable parts. New ideas can be adapted from old one.
4. People think differently in problem-solving situations. Using a logical, patterned approach is often useful. One approach found to be useful includes these steps:
   a. Define the problem
   b. Establish objectives
   c. Get the facts
   d. Weigh and decide
   e. Take action
   f. Evaluate action

F. Training for Results
1. Participants respond best when they feel training is important to them.
2. The supervisor has responsibility for the training and development of those who report to him.
3. When training is delegated to others, great care must be exercised to insure the trainer has knowledge, aptitude, and interest for his work as a trainer.
4. Training (learning) of some type goes on continually. The most successful supervisor makes certain the learning contributes in a productive manner to operational goals.
5. New employees are particularly susceptible to training. Older employees facing new job situations require specific training, as well as having need for development and growth opportunities.
6. Training needs require continuous monitoring.
7. The training officer of an agency is a professional with a responsibility to assist supervisors in solving training problems.

8. Many of the self-development steps important to the supervisor's own growth are equally important to the development of peers and subordinates. Knowledge of these is important when the supervisor consults with others on development and growth opportunities.

G. Health, Safety, and Accident Prevention
1. Management-minded supervisors take appropriate measures to assist employees in maintaining health and in assuring safe practices in the work environment.
2. Effective safety training and practices help to avoid injury and accidents.
3. Safety should be a management goal. All infractions of safety which are observed should be corrected without exception.
4. Employees' safety attitude, training and instruction, provision of safe tools and equipment, supervision, and leadership are considered highly important factors which contribute to safety and which can be influenced directly by supervisors.
5. When accidents do occur, they should be investigated promptly for very important reasons, including the fact that information which is gained can be used to prevent accidents in the future.

H. Equal Employment Opportunity
1. The supervisor should endeavor to treat all employees fairly, without regard to religion, race, sex, or national origin.
2. Groups tend to reflect the attitude of the leader. Prejudice can be detected even in very subtle form. Supervisors must strive to create a feeling of mutual respect and confidence in every employee.
3. Complete utilization of all human resources is a national goal. Equitable consideration should be accorded women in the work force, minority-group members, the physically and mentally handicapped, and the older employee. The important question is: "Who can do the job?"
4. Training opportunities, recognition for performance, overtime assignments, promotional opportunities, and all other personnel actions are to be handled on an equitable basis.

I. Improving Communications
1. Communications is achieving understanding between the sender and the receiver of a message. It also means sharing information—the creation of understanding.
2. Communication is basic to all human activity. Words are means of conveying meanings; however, real meanings are in people.
3. There are very practical differences in the effectiveness of one-way, impersonal, and two-way communications. Words spoken face-to-face are better understood. Telephone conversations are effective, but lack the rapport of person-to-person exchanges. The whole person communicates.
4. Cooperation and communication in an organization go hand in hand. When there is a mutual respect between people, spelling out rules and procedures for communicating is unnecessary.
5. There are several barriers to effective communications. These include failure to listen with respect and understanding, lack of skill in feedback, and misinterpreting the meanings of words used by the speaker. It is also common

practice to listen to what we want to hear, and tune out things we do not want to hear.
6. Communication is management's chief problem. The supervisor should accept the challenge to communicate more effectively and to improve interagency and intra-agency communications.
7. The supervisor may often plan for and conduct meetings. The planning phase is critical and may determine the success or the failure of a meeting.
8. Speaking before groups usually requires extra effort. Stage fright may never disappear completely, but it can be controlled.

J. Self-Development
1. Every employee is responsible for his own self-development.
2. Toastmaster and toastmistress clubs offer opportunities to improve skills in oral communications.
3. Planning for one's own self-development is of vital importance. Supervisors know their own strengths and limitations better than anyone else.
4. Many opportunities are open to aid the supervisor in his developmental efforts, including job assignments; training opportunities, both governmental and non-governmental—to include universities and professional conferences and seminars.
5. Programmed instruction offers a means of studying at one's own rate.
6. Where difficulties may arise from a supervisor's being away from his work for training, he may participate in televised home study or correspondence courses to meet his self-development needs.

K. Teaching and Training
1. The Teaching Process
Teaching is encouraging and guiding the learning activities of students toward established goals. In most cases this process consists of five steps: preparation, presentation, summarization, evaluation, and application.

   a. Preparation
   Preparation is two-fold in nature; that of the supervisor and the employee. Preparation by the supervisor is absolutely essential to success. He must know what, when, where, how, and whom he will teach. Some of the factors that should be considered are:
   1) The objectives
   2) The materials needed
   3) The methods to be used
   4) Employee participation
   5) Employee interest
   6) Training aids
   7) Evaluation
   8) Summarization

   Employee preparation consists in preparing the employee to receive the material. Probably the most important single factor in the preparation of the employee is arousing and maintaining his interest. He must know the objectives of the training, why he is there, how the material can be used, and its importance to him.

b. Presentation
In presentation, have a carefully designed plan and follow it. The plan should be accurate and complete, yet flexible enough to meet situations as they arise. The method of presentation will be determined by the particular situation and objectives.

c. Summary
A summary should be made at the end of every training unit and program. In addition, there may be internal summaries depending on the nature of the material being taught. The important thing is that the trainee must always be able to understand how each part of the new material relates to the whole.

d. Application
The supervisor must arrange work so the employee will be given a chance to apply new knowledge or skills while the material is still clear in his mind and interest is high. The trainee does not really know whether he has learned the material until he has been given a chance to apply it. If the material is not applied, it loses most of its value.

e. Evaluation
The purpose of all training is to promote learning. To determine whether the training has been a success or failure, the supervisor must evaluate this learning.
In the broadest sense, evaluation includes all the devices, methods, skills, and techniques used by the supervisor to keep himself and the employees informed as to their progress toward the objectives they are pursuing. The extent to which the employee has mastered the knowledge, skills, and abilities, or changed his attitudes, as determined by the program objectives, is the extent to which instruction has succeeded or failed.
Evaluation should not be confined to the end of the lesson, day, or program but should be used continuously. We shall note later the way this relates to the rest of the teaching process.

2. Teaching Methods
A teaching method is a pattern of identifiable student and instructor activity used in presenting training material.
All supervisors are faced with the problem of deciding which method should be used at a given time.

a. Lecture
The lecture is direct oral presentation of material by the supervisor. The present trend is to place less emphasis on the trainer's activity and more on that of the trainee.

b. Discussion
Teaching by discussion or conference involves using questions and other techniques to arouse interest and focus attention upon certain areas, and by doing so creating a learning situation. This can be one of the most

valuable methods because it gives the employees an opportunity to express their ideas and pool their knowledge.

    c. Demonstration
The demonstration is used to teach how something works or how to do something. It can be used to show a principle or what the results of a series of actions will be. A well-staged demonstration is particularly effective because it shows proper methods of performance in a realistic manner.

    d. Performance
Performance is one of the most fundamental of all learning techniques or teaching methods. The trainee may be able to tell how a specific operation should be performed but he cannot be sure he knows how to perform the operation until he has done so.
As with all methods, there are certain advantages and disadvantages to each method.

    e. Which Method to Use
Moreover, there are other methods and techniques of teaching. It is difficult to use any method without other methods entering into it. In any learning situation, a combination of methods is usually more effective than any one method alone.

Finally, evaluation must be integrated into the other aspects of the teaching-learning process.

It must be used in the motivation of the trainees; it must be used to assist in developing understanding during the training; and it must be related to employee application of the results of training.

This is distinctly the role of the supervisor.

www.ingramcontent.com/pod-product-compliance
Lightning Source LLC
Chambersburg PA
CBHW082045300426
44117CB00015B/2614